Down With Rules

Down With Rules

SUMIRASKO

PARTRIDGE

A Penguin Random House Company

To order additional copies of this book, contact
Partridge India
000 800 10062 62
orders.india@partridgepublishing.com

www.partridgepublishing.com/india

Contents

Strange Choices

At the beginning I want you to laugh
    at the end you all must weep
    Weep and cry (tears of real joy)
    if you don't I curse 'may you die'
        Amen
She was beatific, danced gracefully
lived till a few days ago
    may be she died, for about 'her'
        I hear no more
    (so she was, was before)
She was the queen of the town
    and her name was 'Madam Bown'
White as milk, soft and tender
    She was pretender
And this I so, so
    for I fell in love
        proposed marriage
She refused saying
    'She would marry not a fool'
Who had never seen the college
    never proper saw the 'school'
    Yea! – I tell you, I am a bus conductor
    so I thought Madam Bown
Will marry someone rich
    or some fair and charming professor
    aye! I thought – She is beyond my reach
maddening love I turned insane
    my face turned pale and stale
    They took me to a mad house
    there we married, got an excellent spouse

And only this moment I have
              come to know
Madam Bown married no one handsome
          no one rich
      friend whispers into my ears
            'She is my wife, is within my reach'
I have from her children
What choices they make? these women
    'She rejected a fool married an insane'
          Remember they open their eyes
                          Ah! but too late
yet, Madam Bown is her name
a name, which will bestow upon her name
    for real love she requitted at last
at my insanity, don't be aghast
          laugh tears of real joy
She her strange choice
        has eternized her
She, 'Mrs Bown love's laughter'

Sumirasko
455 Dt. 11.10.1993, 7.00 P.M.

Don't tread back

Don't tread back into the world He say
      'O harte' hence flee yea fly 'away'
    Here the lips are alien to harte
   here the faces lie
      their countenance just fake
    like a character in a play
      at once fly away
    Where I fumbling asked?
         there where the wind of tranquility blows
   Where I feel secure no longer a sceptic?
Where harte converses with harte?
      lips fake come not in between
Where betrayal is a distant dream?
      under the shadow of that peaceful sky
Where love is not misery?
      a day's and night's pain
Where flows the innocent stream?
    in which the eyes fire may be extinguished
a drop of love clean
      really sweet and tender
'O fool' tread not back into the world
      'O harte' hence fly away
  here everyone's love is like camphor
    evaporate in a day
      fly away, fly away
And the truthful harte listens
    still has no answer
  yet keeps repeating 'desperately'
    suffocating alone
'Love is like camphor, love and camphor'
    trying to disbelieve
for he knew, 'Love is eternal'
    knows only one is true

And he the man cries, fly hence
                  tread not back
          or thou will not
        better be not a **roman** fool
             love is like camphor
tread not back in world's school
           where mediocres rule
      fly ahead
          harte listens sadly
    a million tears it hath shed
And knows not how to smile
        is drowning each moment
And the man keeps yelling
      'fly ahead'
         tread not back
or these mask will steam your tears
        yea! they will back
    they have the potential
          They have only the 'knack'
fly hence, tread not back

Sumirasko
456 Dt. 12.10.1993, 00.25 A.M.

I just heard

I just heard the other day
a young lad say
   who prays for death
  who wishes to live
  Now this world or that world
The fire that you cooly lighted
   my tears have extinguished
the fire my tears have lighted
   who will extinguish them?
Poor chap, I said
   a common, common lad
relating the same old story
   didn't he learn anything poor his dad?
I just heard today
   He loved some one called my mother
  he accused her of the same crime
aye! – betrayal with plenty of reasons
   but no rhyme
my old wrinkled mother
   wasted his precious years
for after betrayal with plenty of reason
   but no rhyme
my old wrinkled mother
   wasted his precious years
for after betrayal for a brief period
   he turned a seer
  so this lad is younger

By the way I just heard
The lad has said adieu to both the world
in deepest love he is in deepest sleep
in coma
by the way I just heard
       the fire is at last cold
    the girl has taken her first breath
her statement is not so interesting
      full of topical illusions
    full of devotion
'He was a sweet tender lad'
aye! — he is in coma for me
    aye! – now I know I have a personality
if I can send some one to coma
      I can do anything aye! you can blame me
  She bore the blame as it were a garland
By the way I just heard
is flying high this sweet singing bird?
the lad still sleeps on Earth
May be, is still in love, still praying to her
  But I just feel
    oh! now I feel what I heard
  now I in his grief I am deaf
  and lo! here comes my mother to ask
why I am crying like a little immature lad?
perhaps says she
    'shame' its too bad
  crying like a little normal
  rude lad'
You a genius ah! it's bad, too said'
I have heard nothing, tears are falling
who will them extinguish?
  his pain will drive me to coma
  like him this world I will relinquish

II

And suddenly they have declared me ill
for I have wept for thirty unend
    the charge is quite queer
    I just read in a newspaper
    'they allege I cry too incoherently'
      the sound is not ear pleasing
And they have called a doctor
    to mend my cry transform it to melody
    'And I am crying still . . . . . .'

Sumirasko
457 Dt. 12.10.1993, 1.45 P.M.

Wish

This corrupt adult world
     Corrupt to the hilt adult life
All abrupt
     thinking, solving, resolving
And then finding
     one is stagnant, standing
always guessing
     always fearing
crying, lying, speculating
     And when all goes wrong
ah! its too depressing
     breaks every faith
     breaks every mirror
     situations heart breaking
ah! all pretending all faking
     aye! Life is death in making
Each day it comes a little nigh
     Each day to life to a day
helpless you say 'Good bye'
Ah! I wish I died a child
     on that roof top whilst playing
that had no walls
     happily flying a kite, running
I wish I could have died
     a moment after falling
And escaped this moment to moment torments
     heaped on my breast
in an adult corrupt world

Sumirasko
460 Dt. 12.10.1993, 4.35 P.M.

The Blind Vision, a new civilization

A few month's ago
Ah! said he, how dare you call me flunky
      grey cells you have none
      ah! do I hear cheap songs
     aye! boy – its Maddona in material world
      this is the newest vision
     the whole world is a big commercial shop
     aye! Love is a toilet soap
     you smear it all over your body
      it runs out quickly
And why I shall go for the same brand
when there are soaps from roses to sandals
     there are always findings something new
      these researchers
     this is the scientific age
       we are flying in space
    without wings
     a kite without strings
And the best is we can control
    aye! boy we can choose the soap
and before it even runs out
    we can get a new
ah! how dogmatic are your views
go get some new soap, fragrance your
             Life 'o fool'

I said aye! 'you are right'
  Love is a commercial soap
 aye! Maddona's boy – rush to her
Love is a commercial soap
  but where is the toilet boy
   I ought to know
Ha! said he 'shame upon thee'
  such a hard core moralist I have never seen
 better I call you a terrorist
 always misleading
I said 'I ought to know'
  if love is a toilet soap
   What lust is
  rush to maddona boy
 Justify her love
 come back with an answer
 for thou aren't original
 Just her imitator
Here I will wait for thee
 and I give thee a vital clue
  it could be
Good night Mosquito repellent bar
  see if that is it
if love is a toilet soap
Logically that must be it
He grinned, went, came back
  like a fool grinned, smiled
  (Here is it a soap and bar take it)
   take it

I said 'No, thank you
    I could do without either
about me don't bother
    my love is like ocean
a million soaps will disappear
aye! bar – like camphor
I want a mountain
    or at least a hill
a being who like you is not blind
whose love is not a soap
    to be changed in accord with weather
in summer me, in winter some other
    or both together
said he 'you moralist, your vision is blind'
    Go keep fumbling, falling
    such a girl you will never find
    aye! mould yourself into time
    chose a soap – in darkness don't grope
if you haven't money – here to I give a penny
    And he went away
    his penny remains unused
    love is to-ilet soap
    ah! I am even not bemused
    Ah! what base abuse
a blind vision
of love an unchanging spring season

Sumirasko
460 Dt. 12.10.1993, 4.35 P.M.

An elegy for Doomed youth

Why you died so early 'O Youth'?
  Why upon the funeral pile 'O Young'?
Why you feel not the cool breeze?
  Why a wonder song, you not sing?
Why your spirits left so early?
  evicted a house new
Why your name know few?
   Alas! no none
You too were born if only to die
at such a tender age
then one may question life?
A straight bullet pierced your heart
  you succumbed then and there
your flesh floating in blood's Ocean
  which you could never swim
   the spirit at once flee away
for, some new house – I presume
'O Youth' yet this blood is all wasted
  this flesh is of no use
one cannot even eat
  oh! vultures or fires upon it feast
And the funeral pyres burn 'O Youth'
  Who killed you?
It was by chance or some feud
  or romance

I know not – but behind the oak
tree – I see a maiden weeping
perhaps in hear breast a little secret keeping
a little milk of love
for her doomed lover
'o doomed youth'
you lost all but these tears
to ablute your sins – if any
a misdemeanour never or a felony

Sumirasko
462 Dt. 12.10.1993, 6.50 P.M.

An insane walk

Mad tread in a stuffed town
9.00 a.m. at morn
meandering streets broken
  upon, on which I walked shaken
Thinking and thinking
  walking and thinking
dragging myself and feeling
  the loneliness in a crowd
Men going to work
  Shopkeepers selling goods
boys with their heavy loads
  and girls I followed
A not so virtuous act
  but I felt nothing, I saw nothing
moulds of flesh around me
  my trousers were stinking
the shirt had a button less
  lost in my own world in a mess
thinking over something
and that something is shivering
'shivering is feeling'
  and feeling is falling
in a pot hole
  many or open in my town
And when walks insanely
  alone . . . . . he is very verily prone
so here I am at last home
  sweating, thirsty as before
Neither head nor tails could I make
  Alas! I just want to cry
What's going on?
inside my head, in the world
  And between the two

So confusing is the relation
    I faint in frustration
aye! Insane walk makes me trail
And here all laugh in joy
       all enjoy – drink the ale

Sumirasko
463 Dt. 13.10.1993, 11.55 P.M.

Don Juan

Now surrounds him gloom
       once Don Juan did bloom
My Don Juan in his youth
       upon this very Earth smooth
   Snatched many
       yea! one was Mary
And upon this very guitar in gay feasts
       played such seducing numbers
as ah! names I not remember
       upon this very bed so beautiful
he embraced many butterflies
       slept night after nights
lost himself in the most intoxicating wine
       till, today himself could never find
keeps staring with eyes fixed
       in his ninety seventh year 'My Don'
aye! butterflies are gone
     the stringless guitar remains
the feasts still, go on
     'Poor Don'
has not a tread to walk
     has not a hand to clasp his crutch
on the bed helpless he rests
        day after day
       waiting for death
      seeing the world, so gay new flies
     through the window roaming fays
he is still waiting for his turn
Poor John waiting to be seduced
   to a corpse reduced

Sumirasko
465 Dt. 13.10.1993, 3.45 P.M.

Disorder

Here I see a pattern, an order
      all around me, in every trivial being
from an amoeba to an animal
      in man the mammal
   ordering of thoughts
      an order of action
 all astriving towards perfection
      without their volition
 under nature's feminine intoxication
      the herd moving in a direction
      only one
         towards satisfaction
But why am I different?
   living in disorder
   living insecurity
on constant vigil
      for I know I have a pearl
a diamond pen expensive
      which makes me restless
      which makes me tiredless
always protecting it
      for the blind world think, it is a stone
Will throw if they get it
      And aye! diamonds are hot
         but they are very little
    gruesome is this visionless
         cost of mettle

Because of this "I am always suspecting
    it is disorder" doubting
ah! comes not some faithful, understanding
    changes not this weather, too demanding
Aye! I need a little sleep
    will someone keep this diamond
impart its edge a smoothness
    And when I come back demand
give it back without a fuss
'That someone' could be only one
today it is only me
Yea! sign of disorder again you see
    disorder life's history
a little order I seek
      from someone not minority

Sumirasko
466 Dt. 13.10.1993, 4.06 P.M.

Don't talk to me

Don't talk to me about love he said
She hath taken my peace, taken my mind
       but could take not heart
   love is absurd
'Never mind' if you have lost your mind
       'I said' harte is enough
     aye! said he – it is difficult for me
       harte is tender, Life is rough
     I said Don't talk to me philosophically
      an eccentric vision is yours
     aye! live poetically, live with nature
      forget the history
OH! said he, Don't talk to me of history
      I am fed up with Ceasers
      Cleopetra and Antonio
        this triangle ah! real teasers
      I said 'By the way I see'
          You are falling
       in the Bermuda triangle
     your mind is a blank angle
said he 'Do you think me a crank'
        aye! I am not going Bananas
     just my heart is like them trampled
        "like pulp"
'said I' Don't talk to me any more
      go with a mindless body
    With a heart full of love, your diet
      show it to someone who can require

And they say 'he went to some prostitute'
        gave her is harte
      came back with a broken one
         after a year of suffocation died
    Yet while dying he spoke
        Don't talk to me you all
        let my spirit sleep
        Let me not be put in grave
        enslaved under earth
        but let me rot on her surface
    And let my skeleton be erected
    And let it be written on top
        Don't love
Aye! And I have even heard
        without love he had a child
Who keeps mum all the time
        not talks at all, unlike his mum
in accord with father's advice

Sumirasko
467 Dt. 13.10.1993, 5.15 P.M.

Tiger

Tiger is his name
    yea! so brutal few can tame
yet crying in the rain
    searching for a shelter
in the storm
      naked nothing he has
to warm himself
    shivering in the cold
for buying clothes he has no penny
    Fearing destiny's gruesome blow
no one comes near for fear – 'none'
    a town full of cowards
a tiger they can't tame
    And the tiger is in pain
the thunder and lightening he can't explain
so he roams on streets at night
    at day sneaks some where
always looking for shelter
    hungry for love and care
today he is a tiger just for name
    shivers to ice
in the cool, cool rain
He is a tiger thinking thrice
    before leaving a dead world
a tiger who cannot hunt the herd
    for is vegetarian thinks he is a saint
    brutal tiger a saint
      is pain unend?

Sumirasko
458 Dt. 12.10.1993, 3.23 P.M.

Martha — are you dead?

The wind is cool, the air fragranced
    as if flowers flow
    but comes not nigh your faint voice
      is seen not your tender toe
Martha — are you asleep
    See — here I weep
like a child small
    a child who has lost his toy
aye! Martha – my love is lost
    where are thee?
    I have sent love messages
      to your heart straight
    I have thought of you
      always every moment 'my mate'
ah! what gruesome fate
    With a swollen look I wait
here upon a rock I sit
    I am hungry but I don't eat
    I am thirsty but I don't drink
      from the stream
or, the trees that are all fruit laddened
    O Martha, my maiden
are you dead?
    I am pain fed
Yet, you come not to my aid
    Martha are you dead?
the stream suddenly seems red! red! red!

Sumirasko
468 Dt. 13.10.1993, 6.00 P.M.

Down with rules

Who made these rules?
        which fools?
    I say down with rules
        here a spirit rises
    here no virtues, no vices
        I feel the cosmos
    feel the harmony straight
        no where is chaos?
    I dance, I sing, I jump, I cry
        And all in divine joy
    Nay down with philosophers
            down with thinkers
    when straight I feel
            such intensity
    a billion stars ferocity
        holding every inch of soul
    ah! a thousand ocean of elixir
            I drink each moment
        Such joy can feel none
    Down with thought
            long live the spirit
    Down with intellect
            Long live the feelings
    When stars burn over head
        And the universe is on fire
who cares for trifle rules
            trifle books
    burn all in the same fire

quench your thirst – thou must
today or tomorrow
    or after the funeral pyre
aye! all must one day feel the same
    oye! all forget their names
float as if they have got wings
    fly and sing
Such realization, a moment can bring
    a moment is enough
break trifle rules
    you all overladden thoughts like model
    feel — think not
    or in the desire's flame rot

Sumirasko
496 Dt. 17.10.1993, 5.25 P.M.

Tired traveler talks

To me a tired traveler talks
sitting quietly under a bough's shadow
of a little tree in a green meadow
mutely he talks
of distances he treaded
of beauty he saw
        and of truth naked
The birds naked
The birds speak
   their voice too tender, too meek
      perhaps echoing his distress
from the four directions blows a smile breeze
   and the fifth is by sin seized
on sixth he sits
   aye! tired traveler at the centre of cosmos
talks like some 'los'
   'mute' yet says everything
      is tired for he is no God
        only a perfect being
          sleeping
            dreaming
               a dream
      all at once

Don't disturb him
    just listen to the bird
tired is he, questing absurd
    it is enough he talks "O friend"
    sit quietly hear adventures
        realties of the land
aye! just go in a garden
        sit under a bough
You will hear him even if you see not
    for in every one of you
    a tired traveler, talks, sleeps
        dreams
        hear him before he screams
        drives you mad
in this birth or that
aye! madness if any is absurd

Sumirasko
469 Dt. 13.10.1993

My Life is so deep

I have got infinite moments in time
When has rained ecstasy?
I felt more than one could ever imagine
ah! absolutely free
I have got infinite moments in time
When has gripped the devil?
I felt dwarfer aye! none can ever imagine
ah! absolutely enslaved
Between the true extremes I have swung
singing for ever life's song
    or kissing death with a whimper
   aye! I have been like steel or like wax tender
I have fought conquered fiascos
   succumbed to trifles
  I have in love reaped my harte away
    in hate I have reaped my fay
Aye! this is the strain
    being free and enslaved
  raining ecstasy and the devil
I feel all, endure pain
   reap pleasure
  my life is so deep, none can measure
one can only feel my position
   feel that I'm special not a creep
a person who can stand to storm
   aye! a word can easily kill

Sumirasko
470 Dt. 13.10.1993, 7.15 P.M.

Good Evening

Each day at night
        I hear 'Good Evening'
a small girl has taught me to speak
        what I had forgotten
    forgotten with school
years ago
        stirred again is my ego
again I remember whilst as a lad
        what pleasure these words had
And the same I reap now
        it's strange
a small girl teaching an affable
        forcing courtesy social
She never forgets
        gives a passionate welcome
if she passes without saying
        aye! think not she has no memory
a girl like a doll
        in her duties just cannot fall
Before long
        you search for the meaning
from ten paces away
        comes with the breeze
a sweet tender voice
      Virtually a song of two words
    that ends before hearing
      'Good Evening'

Sumirasko
484 Dt. 15.10.1993, 7.20 P.M.

Point of no return

Flames leap, fire devilishly burns
     this is the point of no return
   in the orange sky, float dark clouds
     spelling doom this noon
My body is but coal, my spirit smoke
     Mind and heart
fight so confusing fiery battle
     ah! too heavy is my yoke
For the last six years, this battle goes on
     is still not over
   but now it seems I feel and deem
   childhood innocence a distant dream
This is the point of no return
     only new things I can learn
   learn in deepest slumber
     beside these sad numbers
Four persons came like clouds floated
     for a distance together
   then floated back as changed the weather
     ah! only one remains
She too may float away ah! will change the wind
     She too will return to her world
  at the point of no return
     I can only move ahead, ahead to death
For heart and mind destroy me
     principles and feelings betray
  at the point of no return
     in my hand is Cancer, near by ashtray

Sumirasko
482 Dt. 15.10.1993, 6.06 P.M.

29

In Praise

In your praise I am lost in maze
        from where I should begin?
    there is no beginning, no end
        And how will I versify
    Your charm is beyond poetry
        Words just cannot justify
    images seem a mockery
        with what I can compare your innocence
    to a virgin —
With what I can compare your gayfullness
to a swaying flower
with what I can compare your motion
to a flowing stream
With what my mistress your eyes grace
to moon shining
With what your dark shining tresses
dark clouds shimmering
With what your being as a whole
a moving spiritual statue of god
Nay 'My maiden' none justifies
        a lover my poet cannot lie
    cannot delude
after seeing you 'O Maidan'
    I am dumb – struck I am mute
aye! your voice I can compare
            not to playful flute

Sumirasko
490 Dt. 16.10.1993, 6.50 P.M.

Menacing

What is the hue of sky outside?
　　　what wind blows on lanes?
　　I can just guess – enslaved
　　　　holding a cheap, cheap pen
"Enslaved" the very world is menacing
　　　　ah! enslaved between
　　the idea and the reality
　　　　　lost in ambiguity
Can ask none? for I have no right
　　　　Can see nothing – for I have no sight
　　dumb, dependent, blind
　　　　a creature so low none can find
Always terrified, fearing the dark clouds
　　　　guessing lightening is about to fall
　　Love that makes heart its home
　　　　fears the being of the same
And ah! this blind fear
　　　　of someone's love wandering wear and tear
　　aye! — menacing a search
　　　　allegations making death difficult
　　And here, Life is in revolt
　　　　　between the two enslaved
I can ask none, I have no right to ask
　　　　OH! I know I, a grain, is fire my brain
　　enslaved, maimed terrified
　　　　　I cannot even cry
'Destiny why it is always me'

And ah! this blind fear
> of someone's love under going wear and tear
aye! — menacing a search
> allegations making death difficult
And here, Life is in revolt
> between the two enslaved
I can ask none, I have no right to ask
> OH! I know I, a grain, is fire my brain
>> enslaved, maimed terrified
>>> I cannot even cry
'Destiny why it is always me'
why you grind me
> So savagely
And why I must suffer alone?
> Day and night thinking of someone
is this love or lust in action?
> too menacing frustration
>> too much Damnation

Sumirasko
471 Dt. 11.10.1993, 12.10 P.M.

Beyond Love

Life is in love
   beyond love is spirit
  Serene, eternal, non-being
no world and no dreams
no flowers, no fragrance
no body, no mind
  as love's search is over
ecstasy takes over
   if the love is deep not shallow
 aye! beyond love you go
'You' forget your I-ness
   aye! pure sereness
 like this feeling of a moment
that is the replica of eternal truth
   eternal moments
But the way beyond love
  goes through it
aye! it's like drinking the entire ocean
  protecting every drop of devotion
And then spilling the whole
  even if it be a desert harte
a harte of stone
  if it remains so
there is the very need of dashing
  your head until you die
escape not calling the harte a trifle
  for a single trifle bestows salvation
takes you beyond love
  in the realms of ecstasy
aye! don't call it a fantasy

first feel deepest love
for years publicly
    then come again
after death or after birth
    feel beyond love
And you will take no birth
once you understand positively
      there is no love
without fear succumb to darkness
    in the serene spirit

Sumirasko
474 Dt. 14.10.1993, 4.45 P.M.

Meeting of Two Impossibles

All judges have passed a verdict
    a single word is their sentence
        'Impossible'
         'What is impossible?' (enumerate)
    It's impossible to live with him
        no one can ever be happy
his sister, his brother, his mother
    his father, all other
And all the world together
    have reached the same conclusion
'they say his is a blind vision'
Why?
He has not spoken with his mother
           for these days
With his sister who lives two feet away
        for just over a month
With his brother only casually
    with his father only poetically
they all cry, he doesn't care
    And they all say 'It's impossible'
Without taking an another name
    I say 'within' 'they all think the same'
Over sentimental, over thinking 'over goer'
    'over' they have given him this name

And what does he say
      'he just stares blindly at the stars'
       in his heart is a moan
perhaps he wants to say but cannot
      'It's impossible to live alone
There are two impossibles
      the former always holding an advantage
the latter always feeling the gauntlet
      fearing someday they will throw
         helpless for himself he cannot mould
         a problem centuries old
         ah! meeting of two impossibles

Sumirasko
476 Dt. 14.10.1993, 6.10 P.M.

Misery

(Misery will never end :–

by Vincent Van Gogh)

From an open square to home
        is a road tough
And at home, in a locked room
        I think too much
Thoughts that enslave the spirit
        insecurity that wrecks spine, faith
    guilt that corrodes heart
        I spit only drops of blood
The sun has already burnt
        brunt to death
    will never shine again
        until restore is faith

II

And here I struggle against an unseen entity
    in the dark pressing me to oblivion
    an indescribable power struggling for each control
        pinning alone, fighting alone
helpless on my lips is your name
        I repeat like some mantra
    Yet my head is heavy
        with thoughts that drown me
This is the point where one breaks down
        perfect loneliness, not even an air I lean
    a devil grips my soul and mind
        it's too much misery – they would perish

III

Yet I have awaken with the sun
        the spirit still sleeps
tired of this unusual life
        ah! with drowsy eyes I see
All seems unreal
        the world and the worldly
      Surrounded by icy peaks of mountain
        in a cold valley alone – it's misery
Bits of paper like swallow fly
        fly with wind far above
     yet they all must come down
        in a moment, to-day or tomorrow must die
Will is that wind that keeps them flying
      yet, the lightening can burn
            them Mid-away
or rain can tear apart
      bits of insecure paper, ah!
          Life of a bard
Insecurity, that poisons life
      poisons to the very extreme
misery is life without meaning
     life this moment a dry feeling

Sumirasko
478 Dt. 15.10.1993, 10.45 P.M.

With a pen in my hand

With a pen in my hand
        eyes ill, aching flesh
    in usual posture I rest
        like a coiled snake
    one feet on another
    the further pressing the window
not a ray of hope
        feet crushing every faith
My breast crushing a pillow
            And pillows hurting in return
    a heart suffering, ah! an abyss
        its a lunar, lunar eclipse
And here as I hear 'lunar'
        echoing inside – down to navel
    I know, the need of faith
        I must have faith on her
And I have faith, but for this wild philosophy
        that teaches 'for all in time breaks'
    this wild pain remains
            with a pen in my hand
        am I sane or insane
            ah! I have forgotten my name
        alone in this universe
            weary of this freedom
        ah! boredom
            of breaths low humm
        I want sleep
    sleep with the pen
for insecurity
        that the ink will dry

No longer weep
With pen I sleep
        with a faith
ah! any day I can buy the ink
rub the diamond rib afresh

Sumirasko
479 Dt. 15.10.1993, 12.45 P.M.

Intuition

I know I will be dead before the world
opens its eyes recognized
I feel myself, my life defies
'My love' now I want to sleep
    never awake
deepest sleep of the grave
not this counterfeit
which leaves me restless
OH! I will be gone before the green log stirs
before any new storm
OH! my drowsy eye long for death in distress
yet I am happy, for in the world entire
before the funeral pyre
I got what of never though I can
from out of the blue, 'you came'
    made this Earth a living heaven
Your love shines on me still
    And while it shines
While I adore 'you'
    I want to sleep
      I feel like sleeping
    Ah! its intuition working
And when I am gone
      then if you love me still
break the claims of promises
      with new hue your life in palpable fill
aye! intuition says Death is so close
      rejects this worldly air my nose

And if for hours two I appear alive
it's not my own
   ah! I rest on only your eyes
  their rays fill my harte with light
    a little hope
  But alone all day long takes its tall
    each day I lose a little life
death walks a step near
    can hear it's dire, 'my ears'
 All around me is a terror
for as they could too intuit
    'My death is near'
  Sleep for a seer
   only cowards fear
 And you aren't one my dear
 I will present you a dream to live
 a thousand verses on the eve

Sumirasko
481 Dt. 15.10.1993, 5.30 P.M.

A Dialogue deep

'My friend' said he
     see the flower encloses a bee
   Just like it
     you are very, very, possessive
Come here I teach you to share
     I teach the philosophy of humans
We have at least three
     Body, Soul and mind
Why you want all of a single girl?
either you take body
       Let someone else share her
   mind
or you give to her the soul
       Let someone else share
   your body and mind
ah! don't be possessive
     there must be some share
'Yes' said I 'you stand for truth'
     but I am sorry
       I think not world is a stock Market
     I have invested, given her something
in return she would give me a share
     or I for the same would give her
     a part
       it's not fair
She better must possess me
     I have given my whole I remain no more
if I take her whole
     I would be she, she would be me
aye! said he 'a bit eccentric'
     Nay I said 'its' a truth too deep
       in deepest love this you I teach
         if you succumb to love

Succumb as a whole
for no great work is in fraction
you either jump from a window or not
you either live or you die
you either love or you don't
deepest love is either
possessor or lactation
being cool in love
merely confers complacency
And being complacent is pleasurable death
So only those live who love
aye! friend, sharing is absurd
Said he 'our heart is like a room'
some one fills it with light
some fragrance
some one with something else 'light'
aye! said aye! 'our love is not divisible
is not dead like fragrance or light
And our heart is no living room
or drawing room or bed room
none can fill it
it lacks nothing
only two wholes can unite
not fractions, not bites
And fractioning in love is impossible
in Real love
the harte hold tight
aye! two hearts and just one mind
together till the end of time
hearing forever the divine chime.

Sumirasko
475 Dt. 14.10.1993, 5.45 P.M.

(A positive ode)

(Lures)

Those days of intense fire
       days of action
When war broke out
      first on a personal scale
Days when they all tried their best
        to woo, to lure me away
    I remember clearly even today
       they first attacked my choice
  — ah! my choice of a beloved
      saying she was inferior
they promised 'I leave her'
      they would give me a better
As the wind, the rain, the storm
      filthy roads, tested my passion
they all blocked the path
     a ten feet high wall
    Aye! even the girl's father
      he came with some noble advice
I said No thank you I am nice
        Each time I tried to cross
Each time they doubled the guards
I thought and thought, felt alone
Against the walls dashed my brain
         to suicide
    for a mere sight, for a more word
       again came a luring offer
   Which even to-day can kill her
      for she knows nothing
  for years she has seen not any face
     I fear if she sees once
    She will die of disgrace

Ah! lures that tempt you so much
if you are true to passions
            you get much, much
as I got
            aye! never in their net caught
I defied all baits
            lived with bad fate
And today I realized truth
            today in my hand lives spirit
in my harte one whom I love
        what more can one get
such great happiness I feel
        on this small, small, Earth
I wish if I take birth again
        the same parents I get
aye! same set of pain
        some baits and lures
same betraying friends
same curses, same satires
            And above all the same girl
                my precious pearl
        And with the same poetic spirit
            I may compose verses for her
accept any grief she may bestow
            feel again low . . . . . low
                in front bow
        And yet feel high
            as high as the sky
        Ah! beyond sky my spirit may fly
                to those resorts together we go
            reside
            beyond any more lures
                together satisfied

And if I die again, the same pain
    the same ecstasy may rain again
this is my very wish
    to face lures in each life
yet change not direction
      meet her in rains
in vicious moons
      rest under her shadow
for a while
      And then tread together
    to the end of the road
composed 'A positive ode'
        positive

Sumirasko
480 Dt. 15.10.1993, 4.45 P.M.

Youth and old

The fire of passion
        aye! indefeasible actions
carried out with a burning desire
        with, I ran, hands carving destiny
     hands of a poet
        drinking divine elixir
    from an everlasting treasure
        Springing alone
     mocking men mediocres
        as bunch of flies
     oh! today he sees the big ball going down
        his frail body and feelings frail
ah! how he is thirsty
        for that sweet ale that eludes
    once he felt ecstasy
        today only life dreary
today they have showered graces
        he is a poet-laureate
    he shams he is happy
        for they expect him to be
    he plays in their hands
        like a toy
     made of a clay about to break and die
He can only find negations all around
        yet tells something positive

And once he did verify what he felt
today he speaks wearing the crown
       a slave of fame
a man who succumbed to world's bait
     Lost his essence, his chief trait
  Moulded at last
     this is the old
  his vision is one fold
but he teaches four fold – never lied
    can still stir a harte
unnamed 'youth' a spontaneous bard

Sumirasko
483 Dt. 18.10.1993, 6.35 P.M.

Ruth

She stands on the heaving breast
    tremors that signify doom
    seize her harte, burns none
    yet, like a rolling stone she goes on
    steps few and the same innocence
     strikes heaven
     storms blow and extinguish
     she a firm devotee
         could never perish
And here the sun goes down
      it's last rays touch her feet
pay divine tributes
     And here rise stars to guide
their queen
    to her destination
And the moon she accompanies
        her
in her milky rays dresses her
      soothes the soul
a tender spirit yet firm
     only such – can the God embrace
She a woman, only one in her race
    Walks with virgin steps
    alone
    Listening night's voice
in the chirping of crickets
concealed in thickets
She goes on . . . . . on and on
Ruth slowly towards Dawn

Sumirasko
485 Dt. 16.10.1993, 9.45 A.M.

Ship and Storm

Fiery Sea, stretching to eternity
      Waves raising to a tree
then crashing to the roots
      Violent foaming reptiles
devouring each other
      in the cool stormy night
The moon looks cruel
      her rays seem to intensity
      Destiny itself seems to die
In the mid-breast heaving heavily
      a ship abandoned is seen
No Prospero and No Ariel
      to night join hands
no safe harbour waits
      the ship big and hard
faces courageously each wave
      lopsided from time to time
Moon is direct on top
      tide is at its fiercest
And the storm not a grain less
      Wood by wood fall
Now near the shore the ship wrecked
      is about to drown
its 4 AM. of Morn
      She is going back home
the storm has subsided
      All living creatures have fled
the ship is about to drown
      And the ship has some human noun
a name erased
      Selenian leaves
        sets behind that distant tree

The first rays of sun comes
    to inspect the dead
Sea, storm, selenian, sun
    all in different to the
human creations wrecked
    hear the shore bits of wood
    float
for children to play when they ought

Sumirasko
486 Dt. 16.10.1993, 3.30 P.M.

The Poetic Chair

The whole world
       clamours for the rainbow chair
    on which I sit
       Without coronation wear a crown
    shining bright
       made of shades and intense light
    A riskee chair
       have in, just a leg
    Yet people beg
       for such a chair
    Work, Earn life long
       with a billion dollar up
say aye! it's not fair for their sleeves
       I must have that chair
And they can buy not
       for it is impalpable
not sold in any world market
    They kick in air with envy
hoping to pull you down to ground
       And sitting just on one leg
on an impalpable one
    you fear their move
fear their worlds
    a word can bring for down
shatter your crown

Your harte pieces, may never again
    never again be whole
the chair may lose a leg
    may be a piece of wood only
for a leg I would have to beg
    And begging is futile
for none have it
    Aye! the wood of lost chair
        impalpable as it is
May turn my funeral pile

Sumirasko
487 Dt. 16.10.1993, 4.25 P.M.

Moods

Once on a black dawn
       I cried with black clouds
  drank my own tears
      felt satisfied
    felt high with eyes dry
      no one high
   'yea! — conversation is interrogation
     I thought so then
  And just the day other
     I longed for a maiden
  at 2.00 at night when the flowers sleep
     just to say a few words
   pour my heart into her ears
say, Save me, this gruesome
      pain I can't more bear
And just a few nights back
    At 1.00 at night
I saw her wearing a dress made of light
    fluttering in the gentle breeze
My spirit leapt like fire
   in air she treaded
  joy unbound had me satiated
And just yesterday or the day before
     at 3.00 at night
   I met death wrote sorrowful verses
      and I knew my end was near
   so I sang a sad tune
     that turned strangely a swan song
   happiness sublimely made me dance
    gave me life my maiden's askance

And today while I compose
        I have caught in my poetic net
a real gem
        a line that could leave one dared
'pour my heart into her ears'
        I know I have touched the heights
these are moments bright
        moods may change for good or worse
        yet I remain loyal to my mistress and verse
until I die
        killed by one such moment
when rose will seem a paper flower
And verse a cheap dirge
to-be reborn again like a phoenix
aye! Moods never remain same
will fluctuations, loss and gain
        makes one deep
a human special, not a creeping creep

Sumirasko
488 Dt. 16.10.1993, 5.00 P.M.

Melody

At night in dreams I hear angles sing
or at dawn when the bird's chirping
     wakes me up
    the cool breeze sooths with constant slurp
     I long still
for that melody
    those notes intricate
that only your voice hath
    no cuckoo's song no might angle's strain
     no angle's lullaby
    ever did or will possess
for no imitation can be perfect
    your original lips
when they part
    only a poetic spirit can judge
Can feel the art
    perfect melody
for an ill harte a remedy
    that at once freshens up the spirit
blossoms, my own, like a flower
    as I taste the spring of music
   feel proud ah! only I can feel
   it's better others don't 'my mistress'
   So divine a melody can an
     impure kill

Sumirasko
489 Dt. 16.10.1993, 6.20 P.M.

The Midnight Sky

At mid-night when eyes grazed
    feeling the coolness of breeze
aye! rings of light, circles dotted
    millions seem to dance
chasing each other
    flying hither and thither
ah! beings of supra delight
Pulling the poetic spirit
    unseen strings
higher and high
    until the very pulse of life
the very essence
    I could feel
in the darkness still
illuminated from time to time
    by levin
eclipsing those rushing circles of delight
    some small, some fat
    aye! all pulling
all yelling to come, to come
And I was there in their midst
With a feeling extreme of not becoming
dancing joyously, hearing the cherebums
    Ah! the Mid-night sky
the spirit flying like a Mig pie

Sumirasko
492 Dt. 17.10.1993, 2.34 A.M.

58

And all this is false

When you have felt the fire in your breast
      aye! no man that ever lived
   that felt this
  like when I gazed at the mid-night sky
      it's all so great–so deep
        fools cannot just feel
    And there are for me no rules
        Where I stand is a place holy
   Shivering ecstasy bestows destiny
      aye! a thousand restless night
 is not too high a price
      for a moment of supreme delight
 of vision from such a height
      aye! how I danced in joy
Shimmering like the stars from head to toe
   not like these millions insects creeping
      Creeping slow–slow
A feeling extreme of not becoming
      but being
   ah! a crowned king
      wearing stars
And I say all this is false
    Will appear so
When you have no divine eyes to see
   And poetic ears to hear
Ah! when you are creature low

Sumirasko
493 Dt. 17.10.1993, 5.00 P.M.

The Tree

I feel the tree
              standing close to it
rough barks seem melting cold
              the tree a decade old
aye! I see the fire
              burning the bark, feel it
                     to be mine
              ah! burning tree how divine
And roots so deep
              aye! they burn too
the tree and me
       Who is who? I cannot see
just feel how the fiery leaves
              talk to me
their talk is their motion
              aye! such joyful meeting
              a salvation
       Rhythmic life, throbbing pulse
              sublime fire
fiery air
              everywhere
ah! fiery air the very consciousness
              is fair

fiery air, fiery tree, fiery me
     all one
aye! they all laugh when I do
    they all dance with me
I feel I am the tree
     divine merriment
my eyes close
     as I might finally fire to fire
unquenched left
    is no desire

Sumirasko
495 Dt. 17.10.1993, 5.10 P.M.

Just your grace

I am proud of myself
      proud of you 'o girl'
can match no hellish pain
      this life a pearl
what diamonds I possess
      when I have you in my embrace
And the bonfire seems pleasant
      even if it kills me each moment
Who is so fortunate
      in this material world
to be three at once
      three — the supreme being
a philosopher, a poet, a lover
      And all these
      passionately
And you 'my love' I say repeatedly
      you keep the strings together
      of this triangle – a fourth angle
      to all invisible
      like air – but vital
      without you, it all will collapse
you constantly pull me
      from the hell back
your memory is enough
      for saving the lover in me
your 'love' is more than enough
      to centrify, the eccentric in me
Your 'Beauty' measureless is enough
      to inspire the poet in me
you are enough to pull me 'back'
      from depressive distress
Put me 'back' on the right trail
      not infinite regress but progress

O 'Maiden' if I live today
        if I am Back again
it's not my victory aye!
        Just your grace

Sumirasko
491 Dt. 16.10.1993, 7.00 P.M.

Poor men

Poor men oye! do they feel it?
        Nay they kill it
    tear it, eat it
            aye! lo here I go
    With the speed of light
        Shining bright
    the object of supreme delight
            like them I feel
unseen stars
        there is no time
    as my heart melts in their very fire
            there is no moment
    as my hands feel the supreme power
            there is no hour
And there will be none
        for these moderate men
        not even a second
ah! how me they all be known
        stars – like me fire
            like me alive
here around, does any one feel?
            Nay! they just steel
Strike a compromise to live
            Poor men, quenching their appetite
                Life long
            forever hungry
See me I am no prophet
        Just an unseen star
from them too far, too far
        there can be no comparison
        Poor men lo! that vision!

Ah! me and stars
  Walking all day, all life
hand in hand
  Poor men
they would, call me insane
  why yea! I feel the stars
With reason I know me they are
   from such a height
I feel to be, burning in flames
  Like my friends
these heavenly lights

    Sumirasko
  494 Dt. 17.10.1993, 5.00 P.M.

The Room

Here in the room
    I feel like I am whole
Walls bright lit
    reflect my inward light
And the ceiling on top
    aye! my height
This is the room where I have sat
    Sat for hundreds of hour
        Slept at least half or so
but never I felt this maddening love
        love for every inch of air
    passion reigns supreme
        emotion hath gone mad
in sublime stillness
    the room seems fiery gold
I cannot just hold
    dancing I fall down
aye! it laughs as I do
    room I feel is wrong now
is spirit not material
    not made of walls but light
ah! a room burning bright
    reflecting my consciousness
my own consciousness
    broken is the barrier

I am the room alive
ah! with myriad
      just senses fire
dancing as in depth's of joy I dive
    feeling my godliness
  for what more I have to astrive
    all is realized
my soul burns such intensely
    I feel and I feel
    I — the room passionately

Sumirasko
497 Dt. 17.10.1993, 5.40 P.M.

On the motion of your eyes

Today is an eternal day
      eternal spirits burn in me
   in this joy, ecstasy
     in this reasonless madness
  As I go to thee — where you reside
I feel today I will see lily in your eyes
     in your hairs that shimmering light
  your face — an angelic sight
    voice like that of plucked Pandora
ah! my luck depends
    on the motion of your eyes
  if you can just feel 'my mistress'
    how my spirit flies
Nothing in world can bring it down
down from burning skies
    except your sceptic eyes
  So my maiden may it be
      When we meet?
    We remain no 'we'
  I be as sure of you, as I am sure of me
    on the motion of your eyes
  my joy may double
    ah! if only your eyes
can feel the plane highest
can soar with me to those mid-night stars
     away from this small Earth
   a motion, a feeling deep
'my love' can save from hellish grief

Sumirasko
498 Dt. 17.10.1993, 6.00 P.M.

Waiting for Dawn

Aye! here I wait for Dawn
        my harte sways still like these
                bright yellow corn
in the darkness if I see fire
        I wait how dawn will look?
When the fast ray sneaks
        in the sky
ah! how my harte will leap
        with double ecstasy?
        double joy
Aye! — here I scc dawn at night
        I feel it
there is no need to wait
        Dawn always was
only I had shut my senses gate
        And here is the fire I feel it new
here I float with transparent moon
        burning against the blue sky
And here comes the life giver
        here the moon takes leave
Yet moon always is present
        And sun too always is
the stars are forever there
Waiting for Dawn is fool's hope
        aye! how joyful it is
           how blissful?
        Dawn always is!

Sumirasko
499 Dt. 17.10.1993, 6.30 P.M.

In the lamp light

In the lamp light
     last night
Late at night
     a verse I began
pouring emotions making me insane
     sweat too seemed a sign of joy
my shivering hands danced
     like the flickering light not coy
the chimney with soot was black
     aye! but I had the knack
and it seemed transparent
     like my innerself
aye! change not of a moment
for it remains this moment too
     I feel afresh spiritually new
     like never before
the heat of glass only doubled my passion
     the fire my salvation
And the verse if you belief is immortal
     is alive spirit, not dead paper
In the lamp light
     I regained my lost poetic sight
that no easy light ever bestowed
     no person, me my path showed
strange it is – the lamp
     my brother owned
yet it only illuminated me

Sumirasko
500 Dt. 17.10.1993, 6.45 P.M.

Who made thee?

Behold, who made thee
    with such artistry?
And what spirit behind the veil
     throbs?
'O Maiden' each tread
    makes dead Earth a living heaven
transforms it
    Your touch ah! mere presence
you the 'inspiration' of my art
    who bestowed upon thee
this magical charm?
    made thee — what you are?
when you embrace my soul
     you smile
oh! my heart threatens to burst
     out of sheer joy
    you – whom sculptures envy
    a living perfect statue
With a heart unmatched
    even I fall short of thee
ah! ask wavering
    'O Maiden who made thee?'

Sumirasko
837 Dt. 25.11.1993

And if

You the fragrance of my life
aim of this aimless strife
you the wrecker of misery
wings of my imagination
      eyes of my vision
    ears through which I hear
      the divine melody
hands through which I write
      compose rare verses, peerless poetry
    you — my emotions height
      my love's depth
    you my destiny
        ah! a special gift from heaven
    only for me
    you, my prized possession
    innocent, virgin beauty
    on this cruel crawling Earth
    you — my only security
    my only faith
    in love I am a man common
    you — my everlasting morn
    And if this seems to thee flattery
    reap apart my heart
      let me die
     oh! your faith unbound
       binds my breath
binds me solely your love
      your love to life

Sumirasko
839 Dt. 26.11.1993

Day and Night

Day and Night
they look so opposed
one rich, the other destitute
one stuffed, the other hollow
one awake, the other asleep
you are the day, I — the night
    in thee shine I
       in me shine thee
    My rays warm soothing
       your rays cool fragrancing
in innocence thee I can't match
       in endurance me thee
    OH! each night your face I see
each night in reverie profound
       Without break
the moon sways
       dancing like a fay
angelic, everlasting beauty
       dissolving in me
    in my rays

Sumirasko
840 Dt. 26.11.1993

The Hungry fellow

The hungry fellow
     treading on roads stone
  Man hollow, empty
     he ate his moustache
  he drank his tears
     stumbled uncustomarily
  murdered someone
     aha! — for his penny
  he got mere
     they put him behind bars
in newspaper published his photograph
     in gaol he was served food filthy
  at least
     Soup with cockroaches floating in it
now his moustache is long again
     Lonely tears now wet Earth
But whenever he sees the newspaper
    God can match him not
his chest now broad with hard labour
    his pride — rests on Newspaper
His is not the remorse
     And now he has confessed
they have printed his strange confession
     'I never was hungry'
    just murdered to see
     what's his blood's hue looked like
  And they have believed him

He is the most daring man — they say
    He is still hungry say I
        hungry now for the lime light
for it ready to die
      reading to invent a lie
only one thing he was
        he has his pride

Sumirasko
72 Dt. 26.12.1993

Such a night is night

When twinkling stars
            Come right from far
the moon floating
            chooses to descend on Earth
the night flowers
            they fragrance my soul
together they blend
            to form your eyes, your face, your filth
      Such a night is a night 'O Maiden'
            When you I get
all others just abyss hollow
            flies in them
            moon like a dark ghostly swallow
      twinkle stars piercing my soul
            with spears pointed
ah! the fragrance of flowers is filth
            unless they blend in thee
      thine grace
            shines over me
a night that shines with thine light
            only such a night is a night
      achme of my delight
            all other just cause of fright

Sumirasko
836 Dt. 25.11.1993

Wealth and Wisdom

A tree golden
            boughs of silver
fruits diamond static
        once made — can just perish
    A little plant
            tender leaves
    in the sun growing
        its fate insecure
    yet dynamic, living
    wealth, wisdom
            like the two
    can never meet really
            only apparently
that too seldom
            once in a century

Sumirasko
842 Dt. 26.11.1993

Just Smile

Like lightening
        like thunder is love
a sky stuffed with clouds black
        is my heart
emotions fill it
        Ah! you fulfill it
I have lost my reason
        in your rhymes 'O Maiden'
in your eyes deep
        there is depth such
    in your voice blue
        there is blueness firing
in your love alive
    I feel a new life
a new spring
    a new vision
a new dream
    each night I dream
for, you I forget
    my essence, my self
dive deep in love
    as long as thee chose
'O Maiden'
    I will remain faithful
to life, to love
    to mundane trifles
unreal
Each breathe I breathe for them
each tread is for you

Each verse you inspire
    you 'the queen' of my imaginations
        vast empire
ah! just don't feel pain, smile always
      all you have
          all you possess
    by luck, by chance
ah! a lover prays
      come what may
Let my love be your laughter
        ah! even if destiny cruel
    closes this chapter
      me you forget
    yet my love, a shield, a cover
      will thee always protect
    Just smile always
      'my love'
    a genuine smile
      like morning sun's rays
play forever on thine lips
      through life's ups
        and vicious downs
    fifty year hence
        oh! always

Sumirasko
846 Dt. 27.11.1993

The Black Bag

In this shadow black world
            its a poor, poor bag
        once it was rich
                on shoulders of a genius it hanged
                stuffed with philosophy, poetry
                    it called itself lucky
        to be with a rare, rare person
                    listening carefully all strange conversations
            And now it lies
                    there
                I see it storing
    ah! it feels loneliness
            calls unto me — touch me
    so I touch it
        it laughs
And I have put in it verses
            so it might real
    and feel
        its just a black bag
    but is understands me
                knows my worth
    And these houseflies
            that cry all day
    more at night
            say 'stay at home'
    on streets not roam
            they know too, my worth
                but for a different reason
    not for philosophy or poetry
                    or salvation
            But for publication

And they are convinced
    they can get millions through me
So, this security problems
    has come up today – all answer they get
                    ready made
not three months back
    when the black bag roamed with me
    Stuffed with just question tags

Sumirasko
708 Dt., 14.11.1993

Love, Life and Liberation

My head is spinning
      spins Earth with me
   the flash of lightening is in my eyes
      aye! lightening loves holds me
(I won't go – liberation calls unto me)
     Melts this body
Hell with poetry
     fantastic images, slavery
I tell you straight 'O love'
     if you wish for your pleasure
I can drink ocean poisonous
     strangulate this body if need be
        hell with principles
           (But I won't go otherwise)
I can break only, if you so chose for me
     ah! hell with life
I live here solely for thee
     my very breast heaving
betrays passion
        passion infinite
that I have nourished
    though I need not
for a genuine smile
       for true pleasure
for fragrancing your heart
  is yours till you need this bard
  But before 'O friend'
    you chose me forever
let me tell, the way will be hard
    thorns at each step
will test your tenderness

I fear 'O maiden'
    if your tender soul
  can bear so much
    What if one day you curse me
  Curse the moment
    when you fell in love
  Decide carefully
    I have only my smile, my life
        my love to bestow
  only wisdom and salvation
     treasures valueless for men common
    My life's reign how you hold?
  in this shadow world glittering like gold
ah! who comes for vision four fold
my laughter will be your lonely crutch
    against all if you go
  once and forever out of the common ruck
    there will be no way back
  eternal pain will consume your soul
      with only me
    with others you will lead a life
    perhaps easy, carefree, socially acceptable
  the question 'my love' my lonely passion is
    which ultimately only one can end misery
    it's your choice, your decision
in passion my pen shivers
ah! It's passion liberation
    for you I can do the impossible
  ask not further
    Love, Life, Liberation
  Your luck has brought me near thee
    if you with forever
  each others face can see

Sumirasko
696 Dt. 13.11.1993

Sumirasko

'To the wind'

Carassing my skin rough is the wind
      blowing West, South, North or West
  it matters least
      its cool, its frozen
  against warm blood
      I feel it against my ears' hot
I feel it against my smiling lips
      smiling at wind
  Doth blow more fast
      doth turn a gale 'o wind'
      gale thee turn a storm
        take this body firm
  fly it, drown it, in an ocean
      Cool it forever
  come and take it
      at once 'o wind'
I am leaving it for you
      if you love so much
show your love
        turn a cyclone
      I gift it to you
      take it away
  temple of ignorance
      And let eternal dawn reign
'O Wind' come in thy terrible shape
      thee dead life giving air
        take dead life away

Sumirasko
707 Dt. 14.11.1993

Only you

This World, which seems so trivial
        this night, this morn, these stars
         all look fictitious
     these noises from, entering my brain
         cause not a ripple
   only you seem real
        only for you I can Summon
   with smiles
        deceive the spirit
   again this night
      drag myself some how
   ah! what play is this
      only for myself I go
only for 'me' in your form
      come not again this realization
let for a while reign ignorance
      Let me think 'yea!' think
   that the world is real
      believe that you are distinct
Let me behave as the wind behaves
      Let me think 'you' as distinct
   Let heart then
        this night and every night
      eternally guide me to you
      Let me believe in beauty, love, care

Let me believe in all the world believed in
        Let me be an emotional fool
Let me give my smile to you
        take all your sufferings upon
        my shoulder
And let me carry them eternally
        Let me be a sacrificial goat
meek, tender
        ah! spirit let me, be a pretend
ah! let me do it for you
        not for myself 'o love'
Let me wake on the solid Earth

Sumirasko
708 Dt. 14.11.1993, 7.15 P.M.

'Love & Answers'

A fool I am
> my ways are foolish
> I smile always
>> for back home I am
> I glow like sun
>> I glow to burn
> burn ignorance
>> And thee say to keep it
> not enter in
>> a fool I am, so innocent I am
> So I obey
>> a master I am
yet I obey
>> I will go to heaven, visit hell
> Kiss all
>> knowing them to be real
And I will distribute happiness
> share this smile
Knowing all to be real
> deceiving myself
And blow around the world
> glow like a glow worm
but glowworm's faint ray
> who will notice in this faint world
Where even night shimmer like diamond day
> And till when I need to roam
till when
> till when I restrain
>> so foolishly till when?

Sumirasko
700 Dt. 14.11.1993

The Escape

The World is dull, the World is ugly
the world is vicious, the world is static
changes are superficial, the world is dogmatic
            if you leave such a world
            I say — it's an escape (only if)
        if leaving a drowning boat
                to drawn in vicious currents
            or reach the shore
                is so
The World is a drowning boat
Creatures within miserable
only intelligent, wisdomful see it
escape in them own only
they — the most daring
to be lost to death
        or gain eternity
        Peace, tranquility

Sumirasko
832 Dt. 25.11.1993

Riddle

The Sun shines each day
       Sun makes the day
  moon, stars, shine each night
     yet moon, stars don't make the night
What makes it? know none
      a simple answer is absence of Sun
      a negation
And if you go further absence is concealment
  the sun always is there
        beyond sight
   only its rays cannot bend
    like day is spirit
  like night is the world
    it cannot exist
When one sees it in this light
     And I here seen it disappearing
  like camphor
    its a riddle that need no reason
only direct realization
    a direct vision
  to prove the riddle is illusion

Sumirasko
703 Dt. 14.11.1993

'To Love'

Flow low . . . . . flow
  across world like glow worm's glow
in the heavens high above
      in the hell deep below
soul's that rest, soul's that suffer
      kiss them all
And these mortal hearts
      embracing misery
collecting cheap stones
      bowing each day more
in building dreams all, those that are
      so engrossed
show them a way
      illuminate their hearts
        with your rays eternal
      everlasting infinite
ah! back home you are 'O Love'
    but enter not the gates
stand outside
    what you know, you can't forget
stand! for some one else
    leave not this ray 'O Love'
sink not
    blow with the breeze
      distribute ease
smile, happiness
      to the soul's tormented
    Flow love flow
    across world like glow worms glow

Sumirasko
699 Dt. 14.11.1993

With mystical eyes

I see fire everywhere
                in your eyes too 'O Love'
        I see the Earth moving up
                in you
        in your tread
    bestowing care
                bestowing shade
        your black ravine hair
    I see the clouds
                lowering down their hands a little
        Ah! to take a little hue
    I see the whole creation
                suddenly in you
        me in you
I believe what I see is true
    I realize it cannot be otherwise
        'O eternal spirit'
with mystical eyes
    I see the stars hanging by a thread
a thread thin normally invisible
        And I know
        You hold it
    your tender hands
persists in you
    from collosal being to a grain of sand
                And your love
        ah! its infinite by your very nature
    who can dare to measure
                except you yourself
    with mystical eyes
                I see 'o love' — I just cannot help

Sumirasko
686 Dt. 11.11.19943

Desireless Desire

My desire is unlike fire
        is desireless desire
      like everlasting rain
        I may fill your soul
       With love, affection, care
    give your life, a new fresh breath
      each day like air
upon a swing motion of your brow
      my life I can bestow
And when you need me not
      I may sneak so stealthily
not a trace of tread
      not a mark remains
   In from dreams of men
      completely forgotten
ah! in this world
      this is my desireless desire
to walk with you hand in hand
      till you wish
then disappear ah! not perish

Sumirasko
687 Dt. 11.11.19943

Her . . . . . Her

Her . . . . . Her . . . . . I, I am a stammerer
　　　Her beauty is such
　　　　　twice I fumble whilst speaking her
　　　always I stammer
　　　　　for her voice is so sweet
　　　like cuckoo in spring
　　　　　so whenever I speak
　　comparing I feel like a humble being
My coarse voice lacks everything
　　　　　so while saying 'her' twice I fumble
As to by my accent is of a village fool
　　　　there is a ready alibi
　　imitation is not in my book
yet I do feel humiliation
　　　　　so whenever I speak her as 'her' 'her'
　　　　　twice I stammer
As to why I stammer without discrimination
　　　I found this upon examination
this particular case has turned general
　　　　for example
　　　　　　her and flower
　　　　　　her and hearer
　　the last is end — endless
for whenever I think of anything else
　　　　I too think of her
　　I remember her grace, her accent, her voice
　　And I stammer for I have no choice

For loves me much my 'maiden'
    her . . . . . her ambition is I speak straight
       but as she sings I carry the song
tell people 'her' . . . . . her voice is great
       And aye! everything turns wrong
again . . . . . for her . . . . . her I long
        sitting alone
than moving, stammering all the long
       way to her . . . . . her ho ho-me

Sumirasko
445 Dt. 10.10.1993

Griffin

Gestic griffin, fabled compound
        ah! sphinx is but a worldly hound
    I know thou were
       but know not how thou came
    And of thou expiration
       OH! unusual creature I know but your name
   And I speculate, ye speculate not on speculation
    without testaments without history
just on your formation
    What thou's nature was?
With a body and beak of an eagle
    And legs of a lion
And how your psychal clamoured
    for flying above?
'O' unnatural body, 'O' blinding creature
can thee stand for love?
Nay, for, Eagle is forever at daggers drawn with love
   Thou must have tasted human meat
    thou were as I muse
treaded to tear love
    thou beak stained red
potrayed only thou harte's hue
'O Griffin' I know of your existence not
    only today I heard
   And 'O Griffin' I am grief
    that's if you surely stood for grief
Now I know why touched, inflamed
      my spirit thou name
'Griffin' thou distribute grief
    I received it
ah! we are compliment

No more I will indicte thee
for I see thee around
        in each and everyone
Thou may be existenceless
        but the same spirits imagined thee
    And spirits don't perish, life defy
        they proliferate, multiply
   thou are these, spirits 'o' Griffin
   distributing grief, making my ink deep

Sumirasko
402 Dt. 06.10.1993

Love heed's not

In 'Philo' I admire her 'halo'
All the brighter sides of 'Eoau'
that shine in and around her placid face
And around that night like 'soul'
ah! brightness from a different world
   makes my spirit soar
  enlightens my harte core
 As a gaze, wandering in a mare
   And she catches half way
my eyes staring, swelling spellbound
   And her voice questions twice
my deep dreamless sleep ends not
   Cares not for virtues or vices
 When endless ecstasy reigns supreme
   my love heeds not hollow moral advices
to reason that is in trifle, principles sought, caught
   OH! my love heeds not

Sumirasko
403 Dt. 06.10.1993

The artistic temperament

We acknowledge defeat
     we devour it whole leave not a piece
And that becomes a feat
     we reason not
     try not, to solve
We succumb to trifles
     we become creators
We feel every speck of joy or grief
in ecstasy we really laugh
     in pain we shamelessly weep
     a little pain is too much for us
they allege over a mole we create a great fuss
Our level of tolerance is really low
ah! for some murder is a laughing joke
and for some lying is a heavy yoke
So, we bear pain, leave not our brush and pen
     paint pain, paint darkness
on paper and on canvass
And somewhere during the act
     there is a reaction
     ecstasy reigns, we turn giants
     only carving and loving
     darkness illuminating
     in us shines the sun

And this is the artistic temperament
our way of fighting is to give up arms
    at the slightest alarms
  with empty hands sit in a hell
  the rest is transformation
      a realization
When peace and joy dwells for a hell sufferer
    Call it the 'art point'
a more therapeutic effective drug
    "You will never find"

Sumirasko
426 Dt. 08.10.1993, 5.45 P.M.

The Dreamer of dreams

Aye! Confused is he
     dreams dreamed him
or is he the dreamer of dreams?
One night he saw as he believed
     a stream blue running
       on its surface lotus blue swimming
And now he is sure not
     did they dreamed not
or he in his dreams them see
The other day he dreamed
     as day dreams are
a maiden standing near a tree
in rapt in her own loveliness
her fair complexion matching her sensitiveness
Aye! And now truly made is he
     for he has fallen in love
And now his life depends on this
did he dreamed the maiden
or the maiden dreamed him
     on the rock of his destiny he sits
     solving the riddle
       aye! my dreamer of dreams
is she real? or virtual he has been
     Who dreamed whom?
aye! look he is dreaming again its noon

Sumirasko
427 Dt. 08.10.1993

My love you are rare

My love you are rare
      like this lone morning star
  In a blue sky
       surviving alone
  making my spirit soar high
     before thee too succumb
  oh! my spirit will trace thee,
     will worship 'thee unseen'
  For love whisphers
     so rare a beauty cannot just pale
ah! stars are not so easily shed
     and thou art rare, more fair
your face and fragrance like the musk rose
    Can stir a person in death throes
Can bring back a person from kite's maws
    OH! non pared beauty
     thou grace I am unable to metrify
  hence only this I say
     Even thou silhouette is enough to inspire
  a poetic harte, shatter it
     making him aware of limitations of his art
  But my love knows no bounds
     is very near to thee
  My love you are rare
     stirs my harte when you stare
I venture no more to capture your grace
     just look steadily at your face
  the star rare shines bright
     ah! sun cannot compete with its light
   for my love shines in it
      pure brightly lit

Sumirasko
423 Dt. 08.10.1993, 4.30

Sumirasko

Strange faces

I have seen at dawn
    with the first ray of hope
            men going in for a morning walk
                children roller skate
        a youth with a maiden
                only to day
        strange shining faces
            adoring Earth's grace
    A seventy year old with a stick
    ah! he won at the nick
    in a high spirits with a crutch
    breathy Earth's free treasure
            in pure leisure
            beaming with strange face
            outclassing me in grace
I have seen the pet dog of a girl
following her little master
touching her foot once in a while
While sitting on grass green
            licking her toes wet
        no fume and frets
    All around me are faces strange
    faces my memory may not hold
I may recognize not, when they meet again
            yet at the moment
        these strange faces
            child, youth or old
    distribute joy for free, it seems an Eden
    are shining like Sun's ray golden

Sumirasko
424 Dt. 08.10.1993, 4.50 P.M.

Thou were not made

Thou were not made
        to shed tears 'O Maid'
   When whole the world pines for your embrace
        leaving me
     OH! thou were not made to sport a swollen face
     for a foolish being you see
Thou were not made
     for anything that is sorrowful
  only joys everlasting
     a girdle of fresh flowers
     the wintry dawn
     the summer dawn
     the chorous of fowls
  ah! the great sun set
And shining moon thou are yourself
that — I can bet
only those — and others of yours choice
      OH! thou were not made to be enslaved
   never to be caged
     And if thou were made only to age
  if thou grace too will fade
       dreadful in grave laid
     in fury I ask destiny
     who did make thee?
  And if though were made not for sorrow

Yet, you feel infinite solitude, unmeasurable
    there must be something surely wrong
    Yet 'O Beauty' thou were not made without reason
        from your pain will spring a fiery vision
           I am sure love will deepen
    oh! thou wart not made for hardships
        but from these, a song will escape from your lips
    the world will hear in ecstasy
        'I too will hail thee above me'
           though only in privacy
For thou were made not to enough my esteem
    And thou will crush not
        for so loving you have been

Sumirasko
417 Dt. 08.10.1993, 8.00 A.M.

Deep Inside

Deep inside somewhere there is pain
      And pain is deep
   oh! my own I can handle
        but now harte seems to lose control
  for you I have seen weeping
        emotions poignant wetting your eyes
ah! I sit under a black sky
     And deep inside my spirit burns in bonfire
       are ashes, wings of the magpie
Deep inside there is a wild revolt
      conscience eats flesh
    each moment I became trifle lesser and less
And all for I have hurt your love
      OH! deep inside there is a wish
my life could end here
     who wants immortality
And who craves for name and fame
      when at the moment, you are writhing in pain
    Deep inside only this I feel
    my head stooping before thee
        my eyes sleeping at your feet
    never to awake again
   oh! for I gave you pain, for no fault of yours
   its eternal shame 'O Maiden'
'forgive your lover not' even if you can
    let him die
     a victim of his illusions
  suffer not, for his faults

Kill him with sarcastic their bolts
with thine eyes lightening
with mute indifference
from deep inside, a man says
'O Maiden take revenge'
once and for all wipe out your sceptic
lover strange

Sumirasko
418 Dt. 08.10.1993, 8.20 A.M.

Virtue

The dancing air sings a song
  ah! leaves rustle as long
 though they may fall, decay
  ah! virtuous are they
 for they too nourish a seed
  out of seed is born a tree
 Virtue is natural's essence
  foolish dream is evil, misery
The rose fragrance, its smell world
  its petal may fall, fragrance may disappear
 ah! yet new roses, its progeny always appear
   decay is but apparent
 ah! creation is breeder
   Virtuous is rose, its colour fair
Ah! day and night they come and go
sometimes fast, sometimes slow
And though the dew may disappear
  it falls again someday 'o dear'
 nothing dies in real
   just changes form
Virtue and goodness rule forever
  in the bases hearts
 is virtue 'alas!' but concealed in light
  without day, can exist not night
Virtue is nature's prime quality
  only beyond is qualityless, bodyless single soul
 ah! one whose virtues all around
  can realize, lies goal

Sumirasko
688 Dt. 11.11.1993

Strange state

At nights when I stare at stars
    a strange state grips my harte
my eyes amazed
      see still beyond them
    feel heaven
      my lips mumble words incoherent
    ah! o beauty your name
And a sudden movement
      leaves me awe-struck
    Stars, sun and moon
      all shine together above
my ears hear a voice
      calling unto me
      (it's love, it's love)
Ah! such intense is fiery love
      Earth burns in flames
burns sky with hanging its jewel
      my body is asleep
ah! for a moment disappears the world
      Thou sudden dawn
    brings me back – it's morn
the first voice I hear – the first face I see
    is yours
your voice calling unto me

Sumirasko
689 Dt. 12.11.1993

With you

The summer is cool
    the winter blazing
with you beside me
    I just gazing
The mood of the season
    changes with your vision
  Yet on you I not lean
    against your love, I do
you – the pinnacle of perfection
    yet plain
    blanked with innocence
      prudence performing it
Ah! you —— the redeemar of sins
    reaches your hymns
  in my soul
With you beside, — I can't fail, fall
Your industrious attention 'o love'
  hearing my trifling unworldly words
you have patience
  equal to the entire nation put together
oh! you —— the heroine of my yarn – story
I —— a traveler
Walking with you
mirthly on this Earthly Earth

Sumirasko
849 Dt. 27.11.1993

Sumirasko

On an easy day

There is no work, the grass is green
there is no pain, the sky is blue
there is no care, in the shadow of Bunyan
            I sit dreaming with lids open an icy dream
And the dream has rainbow colours
        oh! mine's black
I see her lovely face laughing
            the feeling of wind stirring
        soothing my soul
                a fountain cool
            the blue mountain towering
                And its icy peak
from whence roll glaciers slowly
        falling in the river wide and deep
As I hold her hand in the weak sure
        And there is non except she me and nature
    So we roam, bare, bare footed
        And bare is everything
there is no veil today
ah! aye, a squirrel has broken
        I come to see it feeling
Nay! its drinking my joyful tears
        thirsty it drinks, quite strange
        tears of love that fell while dreaming
sublime love seems to hold while I see it
        think of my face
        Right now, She is thinking of me
        or she is now in other things busy

Sumirasko
429 Dt. 09.10.1993, 3.00 P.M.

Blue flame

OH! Burns a blue flame
        fiery, fire
    my funeral pyre
      inside me
engulfing my spirit
    turning me deaf
       making me blind
    for thou are hurt
      my words sting me
      oh! Scorpio sting
your tears make me restless
this noon the sun is fire
      the trees are burning
my body in fever is shivering
    OH! the sting is vicious than curare
fire of remorse burns invisible air
inside my harte — outside in the world
everywhere blue flames leap
     towering high
    oh! so helpless I have never been
      so innocent, brainless like a child
    to love I succumb so easily
    but you whom I love, I have hurt
oh! my eyes blind were full of dirt
    now I am at last slowly dying
in repentance blue flame burning
only this I ask of you
    believe say not again you are lying
you feel not my 'sorrow'

Sumirasko

O come Maiden, see for yourself
I sit within flames, inside me is fire
see my flesh black
harte's beat slowly stopping
And see my blind gaze
And oh! this burning page
I fear, I too am not acting
This is for real there is no stage

Sumirasko
419 Dt. 08.10.1993, 12.10 P.M.

Cliff – hanger

Delight fright
      are mixed darkness and light
gloom and moon
      a real cliff – hanger, I swoon
I faint, I feel, I question, I reason
        forever remain where I am
      love promises not heaven
        pushes me not to hell
OH! what's going on in her heart
        if some one can tell?
      She is so innocent and no cent
        would keep me pinning
Total brutal is this punishment
      in the closet I suffer
And she keeps like a sceptic doubling
      am I sentimental, do I care?
She knows just a grain, what I did for her?
      not an idle or a clever, a real lover
And she keeps a real one praying
      rescues not from a cliff I am hanging
The Psycho says women enjoy this too much
      my reason says the same
      But my harte disbelieves, says of I am hanging
      she must be feeling the pain

And I feel it's true
    but it is a real cliff hanger
I may lose my patience, my balance
    fall to death, this is the danger
        yea! a real cliff hanger
    hover around scavengers
        for they are sure I would fall
    I am sure she wouldn't fail
And if she does
        'No one will see my living face'
    a face facing second disgrace
        OH! too big a stake
    a real cliff hanger
    all depends on her my beloved 'truly stranger'

Sumirasko
404 Dt. 06.10.1993

Foolish Magician

A dreamer dreams a dream
a dreamer conjures up a vision
conjuror is himself captivated
      not wholly but partially
    projecting himself on the screen
       then reacting
  ah! what trick deceiving
      conjuror partially captivated
  Captivated by his trick own
    saying when awake 'I dreamed I did that'
  ah! what shame o human species
    deceived by its own magic "Foolish Magician"
    Enslaved in duality
  While deep below
      oneness persists
  still struggling foolishly, endlessly
ah! what silly nuggets
    but we can leave not struggle
  and we feel its a pear
    'foolish men' be what you are
  And know what you are
    And that you are I
  will dawn — if you try
    if far your nature you come high

Sumirasko
695 Dt. 12.11.1993

In mid Sea

In mid–sea a vessel floats
    its mechanical brain paralyzed
nature holds the reign
    on board are men
trying to mend as fast
      ah! but never lacks food since
Won't work without fuel
    so, they stand all night
in the moon dim
    all day they wait
only for sun to end
    blue waves, black waves
in mid–sea
      gruesome waves
taste their prowess
      one by one they failed
ah! the breath they inhaled
      never again exhaled
the simple reason
    locked was their vision
ah! frightened them eternity
    shores invisibility
ah! once sceptic firmly convinced others
    there was no shore as a fact of matter
      they believed and were doomed
in a deep, deep pessimistic gloom
      until death came
    cleaned trifle souls with a broom
      at midday, at Noon

Sumirasko
691 Dt. 12.1.1993

Hear my words

Listen to me – hear my words
    from where I stand
        pain looks absurds
there is a green Earth
        is green not grey
there are only honest men
        'I fear not when I say'
And there is no sin
        there is no sorrow
each creates an illusion
        for each is satisfied not as he is
Each wants something the other has
        and from here I see
Each has everything
Each has an eternal joyous spirit
    Each spirit sings a lyric
        And the lyric of love
And each is free
    each in reality happy
but to realize reality
hear my words
    first think than feel
        if not good then even ill
    for good and evil are one and same
thinking is knowledge
        freedom is feeling it
the former is light
(the former is discovering wand
    the latter is healing)

Which burns the illusionary fetter
that enslaves thee
from this plane verily this, I see

Sumirasko
425 Dt. 08.10.1993, 5.15 P.M.

After wind and storm

From chaos
    After wind and storm
        peace is born
    And not a simple one
        not dull moments
    after a compromising agreement
        but a livelier one
    full of deep emotional sentiments
            sentiments that I feel will stay
    come what may
        cyclones, hurricanes or samoom
    love will never decay
will shine forever my mistress face
like it sparkles now
shallow misunderstandings will never our spirits cow
will never break any bough
of our love is tree now mature
And the tree itself will be uprooted not
        till eternity
for its root are so real, can judge not
           humanity
           the green leaves sparkle
        the fruits taste sweet
    ah! a heavenly treat
    After wind and storm
    more festive is its light head form
    her angelic look, my faith adorns

Sumirasko
434 Dt. 09.10.1993

Fire

My (soul) thou have touched
    that lovely stately height
from whence everything looks fiery
    but there is no fright
    My (soul) thou burn, thyself
    with that strange sensation
And I feel something strange
    something heightening my range
My (soul) now if both burn more bright
    my heart will burst with joy
    blood will stain mother earth
    'O Soul wait, no more mirth'
No more this high romance
    stay stable in short flames
big fire of joy may melt me
    may free me completely
My 'soul why this impatience?'
    keep burning steadily
until the funeral pile fires
    make thee free readily

Sumirasko
428 Dt. 08.10.1993, 6.18 P.M.

Never I hoped

Dreams of yesterday
    'a maiden loveful, love faithful'
    are fulfilled today
    ah! never I hoped
        in my life would come such day
    (Ah! illusions too are beatific)
    Will be mine a beautiful fay
        and salvation – never I hoped for that
    immortality meant
        just a name remembered
    remembered for ages
        on books printed, finding
            a place in historical pages
    Never I hoped
        I could escaped from the crushing mill
    mania, depression smothering me
Never I hoped, for poetry
        it came in
Never I hoped my love being ever required?
        and I got love overwhelming
Never I hoped for salvation
        I realized it
Never I hoped of waking up
        I woke up
ah! from my experience
        thee can draw a conclusion
    right or wrong
    when you hope for nothing
            you get nothing
        only that which you are you know
        not a grain less, not a grain more

Sumirasko
693 Dt. 12.11.1993

Sumirasko

On a clear sunny day

The flowers that shine
     ah! their reflection in flowing brook
     clear transparent
ah! Life lifts soul
     Life is fragranceful
     Life potrays love
Life feel I
     in the air blowing
Your breath 'o fay'
     in the warmth of rays
Your love's heat
     all seems well, all is well
     on a clear sunny day
As I close my eyes
     dots of light dance in front
move, hither, thither
     ah! how they run!
I fetch them, show them in a pattern
     ah! your face blossoms in front
Your eyes black, your lips red
     ah! all so clear
     so clear an imagination
     extreme of passion
sitting with face towards the sun
     make its journey to distant horizon
ah! a clear vision bestows its rays
     is so near your pretty face
     sitting leisurely ah! may the day stay
     for life is life on a clear sunny day
     more than . . . . .

Sumirasko
682 Dt. 10.01.1993

High Romance

The field dancing with joy
  amidst yellow corn dances a boy
 touching every leaf, feeling it
 ah! touching fire burning sky
his foot wavers, his hand move up
  running alone at mid day
 in ever stretching feeling titled Earth
 alone with nature, what mirth!?
He sees the sky blue
  he feels the blueness
 he sees, the white water-dogs
  he feels their whiteness
 His small treads measuring
   the vast tracts
  dust and Earth
   adoring his buttonless shirt
Ah! don't you commit an error
  go see your face in the mirror
 does your face is as fresh
  if it is only then pity him
Call him poor
  he is more never to the prime – mover
 dynamic in his dance
  he is the high romance

Sumirasko
680 Dt. 10.11.1993

A Scientific Catastrophe

**(Mount Galeras Jan. 1993, Pasta City
N of Colombia 10 Scientist — 6 Killed,
    4 burn (unspecified injuries)**

They sat to discuss
        ah! natures cruel work
they went to investigate
        — the Volcano, the Crater
ten intellectual giants
        — moved stealthily armed
with knowledge
        to unravel natures mystery
Ah! they descended in about
        two to be sure
    ah! nature descended then and there
she would teach them, not a game fair
fountain of red fury
        reduced them to cinders
ah! how they felt, even a reflex before
        body melting like wax
ah! Nature mother
        permitted not her sons
ah! a prey of molten mystery
        erratic, eccentric, insanely explosion
a catastrophe for scientific exploration
            breaker of ambitions
    the volcano unpredictable
            engulfing those who predict
    ah! what great reminder
            against nature
human mind is still a pygmy

And forget not 'o man'
      these we want to conquer
essentially turn our enemy
      Nature — she is no exception
you cannot seize her, direct her
      ah! its just a little brute lesion.

Sumirasko
682 Dt. 11.11.1993

From real to love real

My heaven is locked up
    My flight is over
inside the castle I've come
yet, I fly
    aha! you see my outside
There is no mind, no hand, no pen
still I write
you are me
    yet for you I crave
      crave all day
for you I crave for you
it feels like the first breeze
of spring
Everything is new
stable
    not ephemeral
aha! Earth is heavenly
    embellished is love
emerald studded
    What is this era!
    What is this age!
your face I see carved
    on each page
as I turn this love's book
    oh! even at mid-night
so devoted is my heart

your name is its even song
oh! for you I long
long all along
whole day, not a minute less
ah! to behold your face graceful
graceful

Sumirasko
854 Dt. 28.11.1993

The River

From the bank's I stare
    at the immense expanse of tears
flowing steadily
    shining tears, sparkling stars
messengers of nature's joy
    oh! nature herself flows
What beauty bestows
    with a River what life will be?
Ah! when you behold
    upon her heaving breast
    (not tired she is)
Ships, boats, green leaves and all
swept away blindly
    without any resistance
With the current
    you know she symbolizes love
Ah! the river
    reflecting the firmament's above
be it Sun's majestic glance
    or moon's sky askance
    or stars dim shimmer
She reflects all, never distorts
    like a plane mirror
going on and on, like life is River
    sometimes cool and at times
    suffering from a mild fever
    still flowing
    joyously flowing

Sumirasko
661 Dt. 08.11.1993

Why

Gently I opened my eyes
      ah! upon touch of a feather
   shining rays beakoned me
      Ah! dawn wake me up
   from deep slumber
      Where dreams cannot break in
   only soothing hollowness persists
      neither pain nor pleasure
      neither darkness nor light
   smiling I ask nature
ah! why now she makes me drowsy
      captivated by her enchantine beauty
ah! I was alive their fully
      awake in dreamless sleep
why I dream again the world?
why I sleep again?
Why I move to watch my face?
      laughingly I ask destroy
   I know their secret
      And who says dawn wake-up
   ah! I dream now, that I have woken up

I know I dream you 'O Dawn'
    oh! whom you entice
With your rays 'O Sun'
    Whom you order to arise?
    me!
aye! what play is this?
    in sleep I work
O awoke I rest
    oh! dream work
they neither take me high, not low
    can illusions anything bestow
from this life a dream
    why also much hope?
    Why?

Sumirasko
679 Dt. 10.11.1993

When emotions erupt

When emotions erupt
        quite abrupt
    I seize my harte with both hands
        ah! dormant passions
    when is activated
        love burns up like a Volcano
            love flows as love
    only sweet and soothing
        ah! it seems in moments such
    ah! I can live without breathing
        without a breath I am
    when emotions erupt
            solely swept away
            by love, love
The green grass looks green
        the black sky, blacker
    the clouds I feel cool as ice
        as they burst
    I hear your name echoing 'o love'
        as the fire leaps
    I see your face beatific

I weave such fantasies 'o love'
    flying like a dove
When emotions erupt
    heaven turns this world
alive throbbing not dead
    dancing like my tread
Wavering in ecstasy
    my spirit leaps
ah! when emotions erupt
    there is no 'if', there is no 'but'
      one we are 'o love'
        remains no trifle wide gulf

Sumirasko
663 Dt. 08.11.1993

Conquest

The Earth depends on Sun
       or Sun on Earth
    the body depends on spirit
       or spirit on body
    if you know – you know
    if you express in one's favour
you know not – only you are clever
if you prove both ways
    with logic double – edged
or abondon enraged
or a simple nod meaning less
ah! fools, you aren't a sage
    I keep my breath to myself
And say if you can believe
    or better you can understand
'I create the world and eat it up'
    only questions I leave
if you realize them, yours is the conquest
    Am I hungry 'o souls'
    can I be?
      in any sense whatsoever
I thou'st whom you seek
    can I like you 'mortals'
    create and destroy
Can I have virtues and vices?
   am I eternal or non–eternal?

And if I be infinite or too have a limit
    And if I be infinite
        Am I not you?
And if I am you
    who depends on whom
        the Sun on Earth
    or Earth on Sun
        spirit on body
    or body on spirit
if its clear – yours is conquest
if its rot – its the same rot
        your birth is wasted
    though you can take birth not

Sumirasko
659 Dt. 08.11.1993

Folk Song

At mid night
                on coal tar roads
        I trod
                too fast on my way to home
    in the cool breeze fluttered my shirt
                like a kite
    in the darkness my eyes stared
                for a ray of light
    And ears starved for human voice
            I trod and trod
    passed many sleeping men
                lost in dreams
    a sudden melody stirred my soul
from too far it came
    yet, ten paces and near it was
    clear sonorous
            like the clear night
From a building half constructed
            it came
perhaps, labourers song
    ah! so happily at mid – night
a folk song
    quite alien words
for a town dweller
like a thief I stole their happiness
    shared their mood elated
            in ecstasy, profound
    it seemed on air I stood
            not on some solid ground

And suddenly it stopped
   all of a sudden
'the folk song, the folk song'
   I muttered
thinking of the village fire
   and the group sitting around it singing
the vision came, till this very moment
     it hugs me
ah! Folk song its a dimension another
    so close to heart, so soothing
      so natural so passion arousing
  And can one feel that way I felt
  on city street hearing a folk song
    what! welcome change

Sumirasko
665 Dt. 08.11.1993

Love – Poem

Reciting a verse
    in her presence
oh! how my voice trembles?
    how my eyes flash?
ah! too unsure of the impact
    reading her face like a flower
calculating, waiting
    pouring heart in every word
    ah! a strange feeling
      of never quite succeeding
    yet never knowing
       what is missing?
perhaps something indescribable
       gloriously impalpable
that even know not I
yet Ah! whilst I recite
forgetting myself
    the atmosphere, the air
stirs with love
    its depths I feel more intensely then ever
sitting beside her
    in rapt in verses
for a while I forget I sit on a chair
    Ah! I recite a love – poem
      as one offers to the Goddess a prayer
is lost on her – the devotee
no long a poetic fantasy
    only burning truth laid bare

Sumirasko
669 Dt. 08.11.1993

At all times

At all times so clear is my mind
         I feel you 'o innocent'
   in moments each
      in heart you I find
   see your face smiling 'o smile'
        at all times
      making my heart leap a little
  ah! love I can feel it
When the sun goes down, the moon comes up
      or when says Adieu
   dawn wakes up 'O Dawn'
     at all times you remain the same
Whether I read some novel 'o noble'
     or walk in the open air
   or do something other, at all times
     I can feel you near
In this world of imagination 'o real'
   when I come
  ah! your grace I feel 'O Beauty'
   as none other can
At all times in whatever clime
   you bind me 'o big hearted'
 your love is my life
   ah! this life, these lives, your alm

Sumirasko
673 Dt. 09.11.1993

Love cannot take you

Love cannot take you
        where this feeling can
    ah! it can bestow only smiles
        but what not this feeling can
The feeling of deep blissful solitude
        like that of deep oceans
    ah! love knows only the waves
        changes its hue with seasons
shines in day, shines at night
        ah! in what different lights
    deep inside there is unchanging darkness
        ah! solitude is blissness
            is bliss it self
Ah! love can betray
        solitude cannot, never nay
Two! create a conflict decent
        solitude ah! is complacent
so follow me if you like
        where love cannot take you
follow me but know
        even I cannot take you
        (for I am you)
who knows this really knows
though nothing to others he owes
Love then is not forced virtue
    is consciousness of a solitary status

Sumirasko
679 Dt. 09.11.1993

Rescuer

In this cold winter dire
  your love is like fire
 soothing my soul
  not a part but whole
Eternal warmeth
  bestows your charm
 your very passion
  my yoke lessons
Ah! this dead night
  only you make it alive
 without thee
  what will be like this shadow life
'O Rescuer' your love's fire
  shines in me like ray
 may it lessen not
  oh! to you 'I pray'
only The fire that burns
  may it turn as cold as ice
 when comes summer
  burns my body at mid–day

Sumirasko
678 Dt. 10.11.1993

Peerless Peer

We choose the wrong ones
    if we have the alternatives
  And no choice we have
    yet see our folly
      we believe we have one
      feel comfortable that way
    restricted to Two hundred shades
  We never look beyond
      we fumble one day
        fall on the ground
    still enter headlong in the grave
    for matters not
      what choices you make
  A slave's choice has no meaning
      the master sits overhead
      And unless
    you realize him
      by any means
your choices remain meaningless
    Each a new fault
  to an endless series of faults
    your birth was first
Now take refuge
  in God's embrace
shun all stick to one
  And realize you are him
faults turn virtue if he wishes
    if you be faithful, you turn him
    your faults disappear
    you turn a peer
      peerless peer

Sumirasko
93 Dt. 28.12.1993

First Lines

On her shoulders rests my head
       nostrils filled up with a sweet fragrance
And my soul rests under her shadow
       under her black, black tresses
yet resting it leaps
       ah! its love special not creep
there is stillness around
       Where we sit is no hunting ground
But a garden special
       blossoming flowers in spring
Listen to the bees song
       Coming nigh . . . . a faint, faint humming
Drinking as I drink from her eyes
       love's sweet nectar
feel the fullness of existence
       from a distance
Life has just begun
       a few minutes before
in her shadow
       these first lines I wrote

Sumirasko
443 Dt. 10.10.1993, 5.00 P.M.

Lord's Grace

'O' omnipotent
           active and latent
                at once
           powerful and meek
                at once
           destroyer and saviour
                at once
     We pray to thee
           We always see thou
     in beauty and ugliness
     in cowardice, in manliness
     in abundance, in famine
     in nights black darkness
           in days soothing ray
     in despair, in hope
           all we accept, Never say 'No'
accept without any word
           sufferings you bestow
     accept pleasure and fortune
           or else what you give as alms
     to us 'beggars'
           though we not beg
     O Lord great is your grace
           beyond us base
OH! To you we pray – pray
           Just for prayer's sake
     your laws we obey
           beyond our reason

O Lord thou art just
    thou deal such in equivocations
ah! your depth, your grace
    is beyond even our imagination
your grace is such 'O Lord'
    blind we follow
the way your love shows
    oh! this life to you we owe
Father in front of thee we bow

Sumirasko
656 Dt. 07.11.1993

Beauty beautiful

Your single gaze
      has burnt my past book's pages
   even ashes no longer remain
      to stuff my memory
   my life begins with you
      will end with you this story
The Earth and stars
      may quarrely, enviously
or the moon
      may turn pale
or from same 'Celestial World'
      may descend a fairy
only to you I belong still
      you – who has a kind way of enduring

Sumirasko
654 Dt. 07.11.1993

Foolishly wise

When the stars shine
       he says 'they wink'
When the wet moon saunters
       he says 'treads his beloved'
When the sun awakes him
       he says 'he now sleeps'
all day he keeps smiling
       says words non understand
they fear his stand
so he now talks not at all
And when he is quiet
       they fear 'he is going to die'
only he smiles, smiles, smiles
       says 'he sees the spirit behind the veil'
       they turn pale
         he knows not what to do
keeps smiling like a fool
he is wise, he has wisdom
       he knows all
       yet, plays at cool
       Flemming are you listening?
       Alexander — the great are you yawning?
       Raskolinikov — the Rebel! too daring
       OH! I am talking about you

Sumirasko
860 Dt. 27.11.1993

The Parrot

A parrot visited me to day
        perhaps it heightened his prestige
    to stare at a man like me
        Be not afraid I will add not clause
            "the parrot was me"
for this is an earthly verse
        'the parrot' I exclaimed
mumbled some pre meditated praises
            To honour of its beauty
        its tenderness
                as he talked in very human voice
            flying – its red beak shining
                    its green wings fluttering
            diving suddenly at unseen
        'ah! he too searches'
        may be for something to eat
            I said within
        remembering the materialists
        or just to show his prowess
                like the spiritualists
            even imitates
                    without understanding
        like the Bourgeoisie'
        I said all
            And thou was clear
    Why he visited me
            a great saviour
    for he said I insist he did utter
            come what may . . . . .
            "Arise, salvation"
        perhaps he came to entertain
            me by his diction

A pendent I said, what great parrot?
And suddenly it seemed me
flapping their wings
Materialists, spiritualists
Bourgeoisie, theorists
All sweet, who come to me
say in words three
'Misery never ends'
And I left him to such merge in these trivialities
the wise fellow flew away
but one thing he did say
'I go to North in search of God'
from where he got that
from some saint I presume
going to Himalayas
And now I have learnt
"All men are following its advice"
And non listens to me
A parrot is hailed as voice of Gods
filled are all roads
all in search
I stand alone on this roof top
Waiting for the parrot of Gods
messenger
its too late my patience breaks
they search for God
superstitiously I search the parrot
for a very, very fine job
To teach him a secret, a sentence
"I go to him the poet"

Sumirasko
655 Dt. 07.11.1993

Living Tombs

Hunger, pain everywhere
disease's body heirs
we don't look, we don't care
heartless we are
         loveless we live
Where is sympathy?
      has devoured us our pride
      or are we weak
         We fear a man cancerous
         We fear a man crippled
         We fear a deaf, a blind
on fast roads when we ride
We see — turn our eyes
        or else close their lid
When a beggar cries for a coin
a little wasted girl
         comes running in
her hands a thread skelten
       OH! I feel
Can in this real, real world
       closed in our castles
    We can feel love
       or can love at all

Where so many souls
        die each day
        Sheer negligence it potrays
        ah! we
        blind to blindness
        deaf to deafness
        cripple for crippleness
        dumb to dumbness
have we senses at all?
        we can hear not any call
    ah! Not human we are
        living tombs we are

Sumirasko
856 Dt. 28.11.1993

Emotional Fool

He was Prince Erasmus
    heir to the throne
  in a big place lived he
    in **Nozima** — the capital city
North of west, he was charming
    resolute, unyielding
  yet he fell in love
    with his maid
Phenoria — a living **Venus**
    her heart innocent
  her eyes blazing fire
    evincing great qualities wisdom rare
Mad in her love
    Prince swayed for months
  ah! foolishly he proposed
    an eternal union
so low was she, so high was he
    ah! Earth and heaven
  she declined, he pined
    kicking the throne, he eloped
Against all, a single soul
    an emotional fool, an emotional fool
  he went with her, he went with her
    to a forest, their doom
When the moon's ray fell
    on Phenoria's face
  She was dead, she was dead
    in his embrace passionate
They were chased with delight
    ah! by angry king's soldier
  he ran with her corpse
    for cobra killed her

He ran to noon, he ran to evening
     from Riches to rags
  he ran madly, he ran sadly
     with his legs shaky, his heart heavy
He looked at her face
     kissed her madly
  'for me she died, for me he cried'
     then died for he could live not lonely
And the people whisphered
     'he was such a fool'
  They know not, hearts has its own rules
     its wisdom is being a fool

Sumirasko
854 Dt. 28.11.1993

'O Burgson'

O Burgson how you felt?
        when they told you about your brain
    a little tumor growing
            a time bomb clicking
        about to burst
    ah! did it you like lightening
        Death did you feared it
        Weapt stealthily
But still you lived a fast life
securing your wife
on barren lands of your misery
        oh! you created
five oasis' for her
        five novels in one year
                cruel destiny turned them barren
    yet the world is impressed by your feat
        you — a successful novelist
But I know, deep below remains a scar
        yours is defeat
OH do you not wish
            you could still throw these laurels
    if you could die, she could live
            if you do

'O Burgson' false is your life
false your success, your smile
go, to her grave
      feel with her death, the real you died
you loved her
        death of love for corns common
is death of life
deep below for you, there is no joy
      only an abyss 'O Burgson'
damnation
      cruel destiny devoured your salvation.

Sumirasko
855 Dt. 28.11.1993

When the pet parrot died

OH! I was five
        when the pet–parrot died
he was green, his beaks were red
he couldn't fly for he was caged
I pricked him all day long
        touched his warm feather
        ah! how it felt! how it felt?
    to feel the pulse, beneath the flesh
    to feel life, in some one else
        It was the cold hands of destiny
        Alas! winter seized him
        he lay there unconcious unmoving
Whilst my uncle — a doctor
        examined
he gave him injections, he had fever
we sprinkled on him holy waters of a holy river
he died that evening
        I saw him black, no more green
    ah! that mourning
We dugged his grave
    in our courtyard
With a heavy heart I said 'Adieu love'
    I put him in, below
        beyond my sight
the sun went down
        my eyes had tears

I asked my mother where he went?
     she said 'to heaven'
added 'he will return as a man'
     I am waiting now, even now
With a faith in my heart
     the pet parrot that died
Will return as a man
     will return

Sumirasko
866 Dt. 30.11.1993

The guy

With all my guts — he the guy
　　　　　I envy
And all b'coz, he is great
　　　　With a man like face
oh! far ahead of me in the race
　　　　And he has that outer stuff
no one can him bluff
　　　　　oh! me anyone can betray
　　　　　so him I envy
yes, he talks manoeuvringly
　　　　　can win anyone's love
Can possess anyone
　　　　　If I can have his acumen
don't see how my harte burns
　　　　And then there is crude element
Alas I possess the refined, sublime
Well! who bothers for sublimity
when in front is activity
　　　And what more I can say
except, for him anyone can me betray
　　　The whole world wished to be like him
　　　　　I will suffer not
　　　　　　it betrays my fay
　　　I will feel not the coiled snakes
　　　　　tightening its grip
around my neck, die not out of shame
　　　just slap her

And walk away in search of greener pastures
        in costly buildings, not in nature
ah! the guy my lonely wish
        for the undefined pain is not his
no one can betray him
        for he feels not betrayal
I just distribute dreams
        he gives the real feeling
OH! If I could just be him
        feel not betrayal with my eyes wet
dwell not in security's hell
        stinking, stale
ah! love will never fail
for there will be no real love
        only doves.

Sumirasko
450 Dt. 10.10.1993, 11.40 P.M.

The Curtain

**(Their ideals are window dressings
the underlying reality is beast)**

I

Savage for certain
　　　　through the transparent curtain
this I half –see–fully feel
　　　　all around me
　　　　　　is baseness
yet, why a lotus no where I see
Why only these beatific ugly faces
　　　　　　keep staring?
　　　　wherever I go
　　　　　　the Demons rich make me feel low
And they boast ideals
　　　　　　talk intellectually
hell with their privacy
　　　　　　when I can look
behind the curtains
　　　　　　know man are none
only bodies of clay
　　　　　　ah! with mind they play
rule their little empires
　　　　　　aye! vamps and vampire
　　　　　　sour round
　　　　　　tongues craving like hounds
　　　　　　only this I have found

Whilst seeing through the thin curtain
     when I stare at a so called man
  their domain is body
pride, lust, animal pleasure
     purely animal forms
in civilized beatific masks
    hell like pain tears my harte
When I see
   me they despise, betray, play
I succumb to hell's darkness
    for through the curtain I see straight
    the body is alive, the spirit dead
at last night through the curtain
     I feel their savage play
   the curtain heats up so much
     aye! it burns up
  naked flames leap
    I cry at the top of lungs
  'what' going on'?
They try to soothe
'oh! don't be insane nothing is wrong
yet I weep at their cheapness
   cry at their wantonness
writhe in pain, all night long

Sumirasko
453 Dt. 11.10.1993, 5.30 P.M.

You had had too much

From a window some one stared
     sings great . . . . . great . . . . . lyric
         you had had too much
      my luck, boy, too much
      Now off you go and off I go
        go fast not slow
And the parakeet imitated
      And the birds in a chorous sang
in forest deep, and the beatific bank
      the steams of Ganges sang
         ah! the same song
Too much is much, I cried
       enough this betraying number
    I will go to peaceful slumber
      But ah! destiny, peace, song
   the same song
     I cried ah! its a base lyric
who wrote this, who composed the music
      And I saw the poet weep
his tears singing the same song
And the musician cursing me
    his guitar playing the same tune
I could resist not the temptation
   Song 'you had had too much'
with the tune
     my lucky friends too much

Now off you go and off I go
　　go fast, not slow
the lyric became an instant hit
yet what agony it conceals, know no foe
you had, had too much reads
　　Now go where you belong
　you all
for I am beginning my song

Sumirasko
454 Dt. 11.10.1993, 6.33 P.M.

My name is . . . . .

My name is (he after a pause)
       unknown
  My case is not known
     only this few know
  I have a little brain
       a little heart
  a little soul enslaved
  a little mouth maimed
     eyes that project nothing
     oh! bruises that non can see
       agony none I can tell
    If you can believe
      my name is hell
My face is dark
     don't compare it to night
  my eyes burn intensely
     don't compare them to light
so frightened I am —so fearless I am
    And all at once
    defence and offence
  I died by chance
      And I die each moment
       yet live more
   yet, don't call me a bore
allege not, phoney stories I tell
     come and see 'I am hell'
   my name is unknown

My case is unknown . . . . .
                    (the person went on)
            repeating the same
                terrified at his innocence
        at his lion honesty
                    I went looked into a mirror
            saw only a face
                    staring into me
            I wasn't there
                I was nothing
    And I felt, my body melt
frightful ran back to the first person
    I exclaimed loudly My name is so and so
            felt relieved
        yet deep below
                I know it was a lie
            the comfort of name, crutch of others
        ah! what shallow life, ah how myself I bluff?
And all who share this verse
            let on them fall this curse
        alone in on empty room
            with a mirror in front
    they just stare
            And see if she can get the answer
    the question 'My name is —————
    See if the blanks feel
            if their could

Sumirasko

Born to Burn

This music is which fills my ears
           oh! how I want to share
    there are people all around
        no one's spirit lifts off the ground
They hear but feel not the melancholy
        of my soul
      Born to burn
         now in someone else's pain
I have lost all including my identity
         now 'I stand for her'
     And my soul burns
        for, to her pain, I am no stranger
More tender a spirit can be none
       oh! my golden days for her return
    oh! my soul Born to burn
         feels her shaky harte's beat
Ah! too weak, too suffering
      weeps my soul caring
    Weeps and burns (more passionately)
    ah! for it is born to burn indefinitely
I only wish if I had a magic wand
     oh! if my voice were soft
if my hands not so rough
so as to hurt her ears, corrode her tender skin
if half her tenderness I had
      I could have sing a song
    patted her softly to sleep
     a sleep without dreams
All night long I could have just gazed
    at her child like innocence

But these I haven't in her pain I cry
    for soothing her, my best I try
Born to burn, I feel my destiny
    her sorrow is my agony
She may be sceptic, may believe not
    yet, Born to burn only this I know
In love I can do the impossible
    with my own volition, the last possible
for, a month which dies in flames
    Born to burn, he blames none

Sumirasko
440 Dt. 10.10.1993, 1.40 P.M.

I miss

I miss those half – lighted roads
those night walks
those discussions going on and on
we both — He and me
talking chiefly of 'she'
Aye! we laboured hard
yet, in high spirits
we stared, at the stars above
whilst looking below
      at rushing cars, rushing vehicle
  for miles two
      used to fall small drops of dew
And that night while it rained heavily
      making us wet miserably
    yet our talks never stopped
      from philosophy to poetry
And then coming back to her
Those nights when I felt depressed
      treading slow
And he cheered me up
      And to night
those night walks I miss
      treading, together
for miles two
   talking the whole distance
talk deep from hell to heaven
on half lighted streets
talk of faith, love and devotion

Geniuses, prophet and man
And of she
together we discussed walking
OH! I miss those words lost
Does he too feels it?
the euphoria of those night walks
I know not but only this
when I am alone street mocks

Sumirasko
441 Dt. 10.10.1993, 3.40 P.M.

Eau-de-Cologne

Frog marched by inner passions
     idyllic emotions swaying at every step
only hallowed face, his beloved's grace
     inspired his tread
A futuristic relation, quite strange
     that throbbed with life each moment
not fiddling love unrevealed
     but yea! love revealed and safely sealed
Through stinking fields and dense wood
     under leaves through which man's ray filtered
And he fumbled a million times
     And ah! Each times hornets stung
Too painful with several thorns piercing his feet
     he at last felt love – broke the seal
     felt the fragrance too near
     stillness soothing the ear
Vanished his pain, stings unbearable
     his face shines 'My Albert' really admirable
She came laughing in his embrace at dawn
     asked shyly 'have you used Eau–de–cologne'

Sumirasko
401 Dt. 06.10.1993, 12.00 P.M.

What is life

What is life
a flowing stream
a hundred year play
an ocean monstrous
      you riding on its waves
  a tragedy
  or else
      Life is a single day
  the distance
  the first — the last ray
clouds eclipse the sun
    it looks dull and pessimistic
      Sun shines bright
    it looks dynamic, breathing
but that it seems, that it looks
      what is it?
  what life is!
    is really is
See inside if you can really see
      there is no need to report me

Sumirasko
871 Dt. 30.11.1993

Moth's night song

Here the sun goes down
    aye! downer and down
here the rays die
    aye! here I fly
to that distant, distant land
where my beloved burns
from my hiding place I fly
    in this darkest night
to light like love I go
aye! — too fast not slow
ah! how my wings dance
    oh! that high romance
in maddening love, insane I am
    in ecstasy untamed am I
upon her very breast I will die
    happily
too quickly
Now I am verily near
I hear her mute call
    feel the heat that is love
ascending to heaven high above
    my wings are left behind
ah! she is truly kind
gave me love without measure
    now happily sings my spirit
an eternal, eternal lyric
    gave me bliss
oh! that sweet burning kiss

Sumirasko
440 Dt. 10.10.1993, 5.30 P.M.

A lesson in passion

'You'
My desire, my best, my pulse
my ambition, my destination
  my obsession, my salvation
 filling my empty heart and hand
  your heart, your hand
 Your love — a treasure measureless
  you — the measure of my life
your voice, your beauty, your charm
your body, your soul
  a breathing whole
only you I feel
  in these distances far
 We
across rough terrains have traveled together
each day I feel
  We have just begun
 Each day love is more intense
 it is passion, it is fire
No other word can justify
  can justify this feeling
only 'love' it is
  pure, simple
   a little insane
  'I'
  am swept away
 have forgotten my name

Now yours is mine
      Nothing can outclass this feating
No Romeo, No Alexander felt like this
      even oh! Never
   Now the sun shines bright
      the rivers have stars
the weather has a feather
         lovely smooth tender
      aha! the eighth wonder
      I have lost myself
            I have found you
smiling forever
         just be forever in my view

Sumirasko
865 Dt. 29.11.1993

How to make Tea

A cup of water
  a quarter milk
 a spoon full sugar
  and a spoon full tea
wrote this verse
  lest she forget the process
She was his wife
  leading a high fashioned life
She brought all, mixed together
he said wholly to flatter her
now boil this mixture in the fire of thine eyes
  he drank it all, a poetic tea
to prove his point
  her eyes had fire in them were stars
And when attacked nausea
 said he Now let me sleep under your
      tresses 'O Lady'
  And if I ever woke up
   ask me for a fresh directive
   on how to make tea
But I heard, he never woke up
  is in grave now
And the wife is truly in ecstasy
  Why?
For she is relieved
  her eyes have fire

Never again she will have to make tea
    OH! upon my yarn – story
I see! they are showing me with praises
      ah! who
  those leading the feminist movement
      I oft approached
   to compose a few verses
one must be they say
    "How to sleep all day?"

Sumirasko
864 Dt. 29.11.1993

Poetry – The New Religion

Poetry — the New religion
     poets — the new priests
  for revival of eternal imagination
    realization of reality
oh! how I feel, oh! how I feel?
    stepping barefooted
      in the temple of art
now bowing, but sharing
      on equal terms
    ah! the feeling
    of growing returns
More and more, More and more
    unless you know once whole
the feeling of strength
    in a world weak
the feeling of transcence
    from the world — a trap
the feeling of being dynamic
in a world static
  Let's make this beginning
    in which
Poetry becomes the New Religion
    Poets — the new priests

Sumirasko
857 Dt. 28.11.1993

Love

Love is living leaflet
growing in peaceful slight shade
an everlasting dew shining
      when challenged
    a flowing lava
      blind
    destroying, menacing
      in lieu
    its signature
      strength not weakness
its symbol
      rhyme not reason
it possesses
      yet itself is not possessed
it springs, it springs
    if not betrayed
a false note
    its form changes
a false clue
    it turns to ashes
burning itself
    is strength none the less
a shining diamond is love
      crude coal in living heart's fire
    transformed
      its edges sharp

Sumirasko
843 Dt. 26.11.1993

The whole world wishes yet

My mother wishes
            'If I could have a life like you'
    no bothers, no tensions
            just books, pen and paper
        a thermos full of tea
            a pocket full of cigarettes
        a tape recorder, a thousand cassettes
            Music and romance
            ah! what chance
    No utensils, no cooking, no responsibilities
            such life full of leisure
                how easy
    My friends wish
            'O man' if we could be like you
                such freedom
        coming home at 12.00 P.M.
No colleges, no lectures, no exams
    still such knowledge
we humbly acknowledge
            And ah! such luck
a poetic license to love as many
        And you know what their conception of love is
            I need not spill my precious ink on explaining
oh! thou art really rich without a penny
And thou take a deep shy of envy
        The elders wish
                We now wait for grave
        We wish we could have been fortunate as ye
            So much near to salvation
            We wish! but thou art the only one

My sister wishes
      O Dear brother I could just get your brain
      And with it all freedom
      you do as you like – no one censures
      ah! no corrective measures
      And how you write so much
          its a miracle
        how happy thou art
          if I could just be you
      My brother wishes, his wish, is no different
  Brain, freedom, praises, enjoyment
hence All the world wishes to have a life like me
        Intellectually superior, free, happy, leisurely
  All the world wishes to be like me
      lowering my guards, I permit
yet, they escape, we could not afford to be eccentric
        like you unique
      yet in their eyes I see a thirst
      And I know 'it will remain unquenched'
        for freedom costs much
      me they admire, shining like gold
       but gold has to prove its mettle
intermittently burning in hell's fire
           too hot not cold
      And hell they all escape, disguising their face
      So they wish yet know they can not
        even ape

Sumirasko
430 Dt. 09.10.1993, 3.35 P.M.

In Delirium

He caught cold, he caught fever
he want and bathed in the river
Came out with a strange sensation
his mind in some other dimension
speak only truth, not a single lie
      People heard, commented
'he is revealing too much
      is too saintly – in delirium he will die'
He told how wicked he was?
    how he lied before?
smashed and thrashed, spitted violent emotion
      And thou went in a trance
      alleged he had realized salvation
His relations declared him half – insane
      a man with faulty brain
they analyzed OH! its too wild a delirium
      he caught cold, he caught fever
And it all become too complex
      for he want and bathed in love's deep river
And so the ineffable man
      now wears a label
    for the river is extinct
      they allege
in delirium he drank the river

Sumirasko
405 Dt. 06.10.1993, 6.20 P.M.

A Hymn to Igor Severyanin

Thou holy spirit, if thou weared not flesh
and wrote never these two lines
'No mistress, wife or sister can be found
in whom love, faith or friendship ever will be'
then the only ones for me would have been
'From Ashes to ashes and dust to dust
if God won't have him the devil must'
thou spirit entered straight
                    to replace the dead
        OH! a million tears in darkness I had shed
                You showed me the way
        Whatever small verses I have composed
                all are indebted to thee
        thou very spirit pulsates in me
And though I now find love swelling
        in come one's eyes whom I stare
And though I have found faith, fair
                friendship and care
        make these not thee small
            for 'I found' these after you saved me
or else my dictum unexpressed
            would have been the same
in a room when my, corpse hanged
                With a harte deranged
        your very spirit, arranged it
            'O Poetic spirit' Hail! thee

Sumirasko
406 Dt. 06.10.1993, 6.30 P.M.

The Samaritan

You gave my ink that steady hue
        that shining romantic element it lacked
And gave my tread a stable ground
        this little social acumen I possess
Inspired each wind that I wrote after thee
        And though lyrics may bear my name
or a Pseudonym when published
Without thee, they would have just perished

When all the world was pelting stones
        destroying my Garden
you provided an unseen shelter
        making me few easy, ah! a lot better
You who made an affable, socially acceptable
        respected me and my little talents
ah! I never think of repaying thee
        for your love and care is beyond measurements

It may be that the 'Verses' immortalize me
        historical merchants may capitalize upon me
And though none will know but few
        you were the one to change me
        made me entirely new
If I can just potray your sketch
        nothing will the world see except love
you gave me all, you saved my soul
        I will feel thee even if the death's bell tolls

Sumirasko
407 Dt. 06.10.1993, 7.00 P.M.

Remember

Remember when you hear my end is near
After the end if not in public
do in private shed a melancholy tear
'O Love' do come with a flower
if not young, then a weathered one
to adore my worn out face
When I am no more
only my remains are left
do preserve my treasure
my love beyond measure
if days thou could not waste upon me
thou at least, at night in dreams
OH! any form thou like
In any form thou like
'a poet', a lover, a philosopher
a self–boasting creature
laughingly, sorrowfully, lovingly, scornfully
in ways any
O Maiden do remember
Keeping, my memories awake
oh! if even I am in a deep slumber

Sumirasko
408 Dt. 07.10.1993, 2.05 P.M.

Wake up

Wake up world from deep slumber
see the soothing beams of moons
and rays of star mixed perfectly in her
in her face, in her eyes
OH! wake up break up trifle slumber
see an angel treads on earth
      feel the sublime mirth
Wake up, I fear not thee
      If her beauty thou share
My harte will feel, not envy
      If at her you all stare
my harte will feel, not envy
      If at her you all stare
at her grace wildest
      for all things subtle
are too for you all sleeping
    Kind and true love
    only for my harte joyously weeping
My eyes too have wept all night long
   in her love I am forever awake
      now thee all too feel her unseen power
Wake up to watch my fay
      wake before dawn
for she will be gone with the first ray
wake up 'o fools' at least once
      with poetic eyes stare at the divine
dated, you will never again need any wines

Sumirasko
409 Dt. 07.10.1993, 2.15 P.M.

All for love

They create, they destroy, they pine, they fight
And above all they betray
Men living in a herd
          and they all do for love
       For a drop of that elixir that eludes
          they play vicious games in nude die
          yet remain thirsty for that deep feeling
          a long and lasting tie
    A feeling that can take high
    they search, change gears
    from one to next, to another
    And all for that drop of love
  Love whose very nature is divine
  for it they all unconsciously pine
  they hate, despise feel proud
  on being declared wise practically
  And the reason, such a love is rare
  is too costly
so they wear masks, shame, play fraud
And all for love which they get not
imaginary beings I pity
OH! without real love
      they can know themselves not
  And what contradiction
    they do all for me

Sumirasko
410 Dt. 07.10.1993, 3.30 P.M.

To a Coy Maiden

How do you love 'O Maiden'
with such coldness?
When deep fire of thine eyes
burning soul
      rekindle my lost hope
So cool how could thee be
or do thee change before me
      OH! I am too greedy to know
So light is your tread, so deep a shy
Crimson your face's hue
each and every day I get in thee
something new
      And my harte is on fire
but thee I see, stare, secretly
      'O empirical Dame'
find the deepest shame
Not much thee can do about it
'O Dawn of my Life'
but I wish, thou weren't so coy
had the courage, to break thine image
OH! if only you can show, what you really one
thou will come close believe never go far
For far from you, air will be none
O coy, coy maiden
      the moment once elapsed
   will in eternity never return

Sumirasko
411 Dt. 07.01.1993, 4.30 P.M.

The Child

I see in his foot, the movement of streams
And in his eyes small, a intense
                              shining ball like sun
in his fumbling voice innocence
And they say 'I love not children'
His small black curly hair
          and his face round and fair
     distributing love free
               only because I talk not with him
          only because I hug not him, stroke not his hair
                    they allege 'you don't care'
And when the slapped face turns red
for A, B, C, he forgets with ease
And I pity – saying not to force
they allege 'he will turn mischievous
               in old age without beating characterless'
Further they remark 'He is not your child'
          you are free to beat not yours if you like
So each days he cries in pain, my blood cries
And they are still alleging 'I have no love for them'
               for oh! I don't hug him
(they know not, I have never embraced my maiden
          but I love her as none other can)

Sumirasko
412 Dt. 07.10.1993, 5.00 P.M.

(When the dawn will die)

Death of Dawn

When the dawn will die
     your face now so tender will die, potray cry
   And the lips red will lose their hue
     Lose their charm to the blackness of night
     And though raven tresses
        turn white
     And not a single gaze will adore thee
       my love still will crave to see
     the same spirit will forever inspire me
       for spirits age not
  my love will remain as fiery as hot
And though then your sweet voice may turn mute
OH! my love, my ears too will be deaf
And there is no reason why
       when the dawn will die
We remain as loving as today
     indirect and shy
Without a word just feeling each other
      in the stillness of blackness
        beyond outer charm
   And when it is all over
      Our spirits may sing a joyous number
a freedom song together
     we will welcome death of dawn
   of beauty that enslaves
OH! for our love is of spiritual stuff made

Sumirasko
413 Dt. 07.10.1993, 6.15 P.M.

Believe me if you can

Believe me if you can
without shoes I once ran
        to meet thee
    I cried not Eureka, Eureka
       too emotional, I am perfect
Further I left my voice with thee
      And with it a precious harte
    ah! too rare for it's a harte of a bard
Believe me if you can
I have been loving thee without a harte
temporarily I have converted my mind a harte
   And Believe me if you can
      I never think only feel
feel your presence, even when I am lovely
    on the walls I see your face carved
on the stillness, your voice I hear
     OH! I neither see nor hear just feel
       feel you are forever near
I know thee will believe
      there will be no 'if'
For over you will shower faith, devotion
     there will be no grief
still believe this only if you can
OH! for I just feel I have no brain
for centuries we have taken birth together
    in each we have been memorable loves
Just we two, no others
only feel it, use not your mind
ah! for love dwell not on facts, are blind

Sumirasko
414 Dt. 07.10.1993, 6.45 P.M.

The Dawn

Last night an Earthquake rocked my harte
　　　　She, my foundation turned pale
like a weathered rose looked her face
　　　her voice like a person ill
　　O destiny this dawn why don't me
　　　　　you fully kill
　　And for my single fault
　　　OH! her countenance became gaunt
my broken harte feels her pain
　　in her sorrow I am insane
so this dawn I curse poetry
　　　oh! for love minatory
　　And employ it to tell her
　　　OH! no more that sorrowful
　　　　　verse remember
For her sorrow is my harrow
　　　her sickening harte my death
and if her face weathers
　　　OH! I feel so guilty like a traitor
I seem to betray love
　　　OH! without her breath I cannot live
　　Dawn do this at once
　　　Kill my soul or tell her
　　　　to make it relive

Sumirasko
416 Dt. 08.10.1993, 7.30 P.M.

To a loving harte

'O harte' why thee love me so much
    splashing me, filling me like rain
    my soul is overflowing
        this dawn it madly craves for ye
      'O harte' why thee adore me
      like Earth adores sky
      OH! my love encloses thee from a distance
          yet somewhere we do meet
'O harte' why thee chose a sceptic lover?
who hurts you with doubts
yet 'my love' helpless I am
    ah! ablute my sins
For none other can
        except a loving harte
only such my listless sins
     can forgive
    And only such pure love
      ah! my dove
with wings to fly
    up and down as we choose
'O loving harte' if our love is not a play
        is not flirt
then rest assured, we are made not of clay
      our spirit shines, there is no dirt

Like your innocence, is my patience
      like your reasons is my rhyme
like your shamefulness is my shine
    ah! together till the end of time
'My love' all that my harte expressed
      is true
heaven and Earth do meet
    if Earth is like you
Do loving you have seen
      And real love's power is infinite
'O loving harte' just forgive my sins
    keep this bower of grace shining

Sumirasko
415 Dt. 08.10.1993, 7.00 P.M.

How much I love thee

How much I love thee?
I know not
only this – Life will be unending nightware
without thee
OH! will not be so joyous and fair
who else will bestow, can shower
        such love and care
ah! I need thee as I need air
        in every body pore thou art
your love flows in my vein instead of blood
   its very pulse is the life of this bard
     without thee
        Life will not be life
     Will be death
        if you are gone
  ask yourself
        how many moments it will take
           in becoming a wreck?
    AH! its your love that holds me together
     is my power
    OH! how much I love thee – I know not
    only thing without thee – I can live not

Sumirasko
420 Dt. 08.10.1993, 1.30 P.M.

Poetic Pen's strength turns hell a heaven

Eyes are red heavy and dead
     as I think of misery
And flesh burns in fever
     as I think of meeting her
for I am not sure I can walk
     my feet are all numb
And my hands just somehow scratch
     hoping to catch last rhythm
And lo! here is a new beginning
     here the spirits soars again
has spirited away this hellish pain
And here in an internal bliss
     I do feel heaven and Earth kiss
     my eyes now beam with joy
     Legs dance are no more cog
     here I feel myself on top
     feel the coldness of mountains soothing
is inspiring even the cloud's lightening
in each harte there is only love
     ah! in joy my senses dissolve
     OH! I am painting
but I am hearing still her sweet
     voice in valleys echoing

Sumirasko
421 Dt. 08.10.1993, 4.00 P.M.

In a festive mood

'have returned from a sacred pilgrimage
        abluted sins and sacrilege
under the blue sky I sit
        my spirit flying in heaven
feeling the beauty of Earth
        ah! of my mistress only one
in each lovely roses
        I see her, fiery rose
in each smooth petal
        I feel her love subtle
in the flowing shining brook
        her eye's grace
in the child that looks so cute
        her innocent face
All is well
        ah! love can not fail
even if it be crossed, pierced with nails
            real love undergoes resurrection
        blossoms again
            its hue more deep
        like my lady's smile
            can burn not love, any funeral pire
And when love is deeper than life
        Ecstasy rains from edged knives
like in this moment

Ah! the Earth dances wearing natural emotions
seeing her so festive so native
    I dance too in unbodied form
amidst blue flowers and yellow corn
    swaying in gentle breeze
OH! my lips cry 'Life is love's lease'
    Life is love
as my eyes behold the white wings
    of a dove flying above
And eyes standing from a nearby shrub
    I feel the same spirit everywhere
      one song all sing
only in different tunes
    its love, love, love
    fest. and mirt.
      ah! heaven embracing dancing Earth

Sumirasko
422 Dt. 08.10.1993, 4.15 P.M.

Now if one says

Now if one says
        women have no faith
    I would answer not
        bring him to my mistress straight
Now if one says
        there is no love in the world
    I would waste not words
        just say 'I am loving, don't disturb'
Now if one says
    there are dark spots on the moon
a fool is he, I will heed not
        does he know my moon shine in the noon?
    Now if one says
        Better be aware of betrayal
    I will laugh
            'has he ever felt love more loyal'
More Royal than I and she feel
        tender than roses, harder than steel
    Now over is my patience, no more queries
        ah! excuse no more, be it's and 'ifs'

Sumirasko
438 Dt. 09.10.1993, 7.06 P.M.

Just to keep her safe

Rape, Incest's, Robberies, Wars, Earthquakes, Selfishness
This is the 20th century fate
May be I am a century late
Be whatever it may be
But last night when I slept
I heard someone weep
I looked around, near my bed . . . . .
I took her in my embrace
Just to keep her safe
And a month before
She cried in a manner insane
Came running to my name
for she heard a devilish news
Just to console her soul
Just to keep her safe
I laid her on the white bed-sheets
And in my safe .. safe embrace
she slept
For years this is going on
I am a bachelor but I have a son
Whenever the maid too, a daughter is fearful
Whenever She is fearful
hearing of war, rape incest
She feels she is the victim

And each time she I embrace
      ah! just to keep her safe
In future I think, I will remain a bachelor
      for will deepen further, world's dark colour
more wars, more rapes, more incest's
      will suffer much my unnamed old daughter
      she will come too with eyes tearful
        softly in my embrace
      I will be at her service
        (blind and deaf)
      Just to keep her safe
(the son if I am lucky will go to tell)
My sole purpose is to keep the beauty safe

Sumirasko
451 Dt. 11.10.1993, 3.15 P.M.

The Lizard

I saw his beady eyes
    saw his motionless body
  resting on a wall, in a room
    today, yesterday, the day before
  for years he rests there
why not any where
    near the ventilator
  beside a big box
    perhaps he likes Vibrations too much
Ah! a music lover lizard is he
  listening from as close as possible
  an hour by hour
    day by day
  year by year
ah! what fan purely devoted
    to classical or modern
    to trifles or nuggets
even his tail never quivers
  Music is his food, so he kills none
ah! a saint is he
  in bliss, in peace
perhaps has attained salvation
  for he answers not when I put a query
ah! he has forgotten that he has a body
  Ah! a lizard realized perhaps liberation
  liberation through music

Ah! a liberated lizard is he
       sitting peacefully
          feeling bliss
ah! that's my lonely wish
       if he were a little affable
    I just could have
       you know further substantiated my theory
    asked just questions two
       was he previously a manic-depressive?
    and how did he cope with it
And I bet he just could have said two words
    'Yes' and 'Music'

                 Sumirasko
            685 Dt. 11.11.1993

Laugh a little

Twinkle star, Twinkle star
laugh a little
take my smile
  you residing far
in my verse, in my poetry
  keep shining
Watch my face day and night
  forget your pain
you burning at a height
A little fire, a little fire
Let me quench your desire
with my pen, with my ink
come rushing in, come rushling in
He was a poet, She was a beauty
he said to her
  your hair sway like rivers
  your eyes, shine like pearls
  your nose, he said what no one said before
   is finest prose
but for me its no necessity
cut if off — I am a poet
  I deal with only poetry
So she did for she was in love
  he took it away
  he never came back
I said he was a fine poet
he had those golden rings
he said it, drank a bottle of whisky

And later wrote a fine poem
a quartlet I quote
"appreciating beauty is my duty
not in prose but in poetry
against prose I am
yet, in love with nose I am"
smile, smile my distant friends
for ladies are visiting him from distant lands
to check on of their nose
he can a memorable verse compose
he had already written one
     for five hundred dollars 'O friend'
'Mrs Chatterley's nose'
the first couplet let me quote
     'Aha! – What heavenly gift heaven bestowed'
     your nose with two holds, out classing any prose

Sumirasko
861 Dt. 29.11.1993

The First ray

When you were born
   under which star my love
  aha! so holy must be that moment
   when 'you' o soul decided
  to wear this robe
 for me to distinguish
OH! I have seen you, not as a child
   playing and smiling
  what miss!
   But still that innocence you treasure
  in these years youthful
   still you dream
'so loving you have been 'o love'
   like a fairy you have been
not earthly you are
   oh! no, not you are
till a few days back
   stranger you were
Today – oh! what can I say
  what you are
like an unexpected spring
   you arrived on the serene
No — you always were there
  I was sleeping
a night mare awoke me
with a glass of water you came
    rushing in
 into my life

And now I rest under your shadow
I look at your face
        I visualize that little girl
'O Maiden' which once you were
        And I let
     you are much fairer
nothing you have lost
      her dreams are still yours
      her credulous nature persists
in the mid–day sun
       still lingers on
the sweetness of the first ray of East
        oh! the first ray
        your childhood my fay

Sumirasko
863 Dt. 29.11.1993

Free Soul

A soul free
      unlike water, not airy
  feeling its infinity
     its divinity
its illuminance, its brilliance
     yet still, yet still
a shadow follows it
     a shadow imprisons
ah! actions that have beared print
     ah! the fruit carries it on
on and on, on and on
From night to morn
so forth and so on
so sure is it of world's unreality
like you are sure you exist
smiles it always at this triviality
yet knows not a speck

can move
>> yet it's dynamic
> Conscious of itself
>> unconscious of the world

yet it does all, yet it does all
a free soul
>> pervading the whole
> oh! ego, trifle self
> destroyed to dust
>> yet for the world all, all

Sumirasko
852 Dt. 28.11.1993

Come clouds come

the blue clouds of my imagination
tell me — when thee will rain
  oh! so joyous I am
 tell me — when thee will double my joy
 OH! see the irony of situation
 I pray to thee, I ask thee
though God I am
  obeying only to bodily restriction
ah! I imagine imagination
  a diamond bird
   singing Golden songs
 sitting on a silver bough
  ah! of love's tree
I ask thee — ah! clouds blue
  when thee will rain
 see my smile
   envy me
 burst with a bang
  rain
to wet my senses
 fire still more my imagination
  double my passion
oh! so I may fly more smoothly
  on the unmatched wings of poesy
 come clouds come to the ground
   wet me

Sumirasko
850 Dt. 27.11.1993

The Gold–fish

My fish has no scales
         no scales on her surface
   She is smooth
         She shines like gold
     She is supremely intelligent
       in any trap
     She wouldn't, dare to investigate
until she is sure
       She is positively fearful
And that's why I love her
     For living in fear, is a thing clever
Fear is a trait divine
     Fear and fish go together
more so when it is gold fish
    Just now her I miss
       I am sad.

II

Those who could not understand this verse
     Just know, I am not a lunatic
      I really love a fish
  Who loves me too
     When we are not together
We both miss each other
Those who want to understand the notion
       dive deep into love's ocean
     or fly high to constellations
And let me assure
      this is no contradiction

Sumirasko
283 Dt. 23.01.1994

Between Aah! and Aha!

A poet's pathetic cry
'Aah!' is bit heard
whom woe and tide, betide . . . . . . he is yearning
      for the deep calm buxom
    Not the flying aha! waves
      Jangling
    like Maiden's bangle
  But at the depth, waves eternal
Look into his broody eyes
they are blue
the colour of sky and sea . . . . . yet . . . . .
he craves not for waves but depth
not for life but death
not for words but that silence
    which evades
he deals in words
    assays hard
      awaits
   aah! he waits
  Not for aha!
    But . . . .

Sumirasko
2 Dt. 13.11.1994

—: END :—